Schmidt Ink, Inc.

Master Course for BusinessObjects
The Ultimate Training Manual for BusinessObjects

Published by
Schmidt Ink, Inc.
San Diego, CA 92122

Printed in USA

Schmidt Ink, Inc.
Phone: (858) 405-9317
www.schmidtink.com

Other Schmidt Ink, Inc. Publications:

Creating Documents with BusinessObjects
Creating Documents with BusinessObjects: Report Writing Course

Limits of Liability and Disclaimer of Warranty

Trademarks:

ISBN 0-9722636-9-1

BusinessObjects^{tm} Complete Course

Table of Contents

Level One Course for BusinessObjects Reporter

Advanced Course for BusinessObjects Reporter

Thank you for purchasing the Complete Report Writing Course. This is one of the most contemporary instructional manuals for learning how to use BusinessObjects to manage and create documents. It is also the most unique, because it focuses on many real-life examples and situations.

This course is supported by the SIEQUITY universe and database. To install these files properly, following these steps:

1. If you are using version 6, copy the SIEQUITY.unv file to the following location: C:\ Documents and Settings\(Your User Name)\ Application Data\Business Objects\Business Objects 6.0\universes

   If you are using version 5, copy the SIEQUITY.unv file to the following location: C:\Program Files\Business Objects\BusinessObjects 5.0\Universe

2. Copy the SI EQUITY.mdb file to any location on your computer. This is the database that will supply all of the examples in the book.

3. Create an ODBC data source that points to the SI EQUITY.mdb file.

   a. Select Control Panel from the MS Windows Start menu.
   b. Double-click into Administrative Tools.
   c. Double-click into Data Sources (ODBC).
   d. Select the System DSN tab to activate it.
   e. Click the Add… button.
   f. Select Microsoft Access Driver (*.mdb)
   g. Click Finish.
   h. Enter SIEQUITY into the Data Source Name field.
   i. Click the Select button.
   j. Locate the SI EQUITY.mdb file in the Select Database dialog and select it. Click Ok.
   k. Click OK in the ODBC Microsoft Access dialog.
   l. Click OK in the ODBC Data Source Administrator.

   Note: In some companies, employees are not allowed to configure ODBC data sources. If you are not able to, please contact your IT support.

The first chapter of the course uses a repository that will be different from your corporate repository. A repository is where the corporate documents are stored. I am not aware of a company that will allow you to install the repository files to your computer. However, if you are training in a controlled environment, you may want to install the repository files. Please contact me at rschmidt@schmidtink.com for the files and instructions.

It is probably best to explore your own company's corporate documents and use the first chapter as a guide. It is also possible to skip the first chapter on Working With Documents, and then revisiting it when necessary.

I hope that this training manual allows you to reach your BusinessObjects reporting goals. It has been carefully design to allow you to reach your goals and, perhaps, even exceed them. Please have patience and try to relax, as there is a lot of information to assimilate.

If you need help with a problem, please email me at rschmidt@schmidtink.com. You can also visit http://www.forumtopics.com/busobj/viewforum.php?f=35. This is a great web site, where you can have many of your questions answered.

Good luck, and please let me know your comments on the course, as it is written with you in mind.

Very Sincerely,
Robert D. Schmidt

Master Course for BusinessObjects Reporter

By Robert D. Schmidt
Schmidt Ink, Inc.
www.SchmidtInk.com

Introduce Yourself

- What is your name?
- Have you used or seen BusinessObjects before?
- Have you used similar products, such as MS Excel or MS Access before?
- What do you hope to achieve in this class?

This is an exciting course and we should get to know one another, so that we can help each other out with the examples. We will complete many exercises, so the more we work together, the smoother the class will be.

Course Guidelines

Do not experiment during class. You may learn something, but it distracts other students.

Be punctual.
This will maximize class time and allow for more frequent breaks.

Please participate in the class by asking questions that are relevant to the discussion.

We will have two fifteen minute breaks.

Gone over Enough Push On
Say this when you feel a topic has been
covered enough.

My Eyes are Glazed Over
Say this when you are
becoming lost.

It is important to communicate with your instructor. These are a couple of
ways to let him/her know how you are doing. Please do not hesitate to speak
up, as all of the topics in this course a significant and an understanding of
them is essential in creating thorough and complete reports.

Course Layout

- This course has been designed to help students realize the full functionality of BusinessObjects. Topics are introduced in a very logical manner.
    - The first section discusses how to find, open, refresh, save, and share documents. This chapter introduces the basic functionality of BusinessObjects.
    - The next chapters introduce report structures and how to format and manipulate them. This includes moving, copying, inserting calculations, formatting, breaks, and master details.
    - Next, we learn how to create queries and conditions.
    - Finally, the advanced portion arrives. This section of the course introduces many advanced concepts and examples. While studying this portion, you will create around thirty reports that demonstrate how to use BusinessObjects to create professional documents.

Have Patience

What does surfing and report writing have in common?

- You cannot become an expert at either in a day
    - Both take plenty of practice and tenacity
- Learn the basics, put them together and, with practice, excel past any boundaries

First Level Course for BusinessObjects Reporter

Working With Documents

Introduction

- In this chapter, we are going to learn how to retrieve, open, refresh, save, and share documents. These actions are the very basic functions of BusinessObjects.
    - There are many employees who open and refresh reports. They really have no need for formatting and creating documents. This first chapter is for them.
    - However, I encourage these employees to continue with the course, as they will learn many new features that will help them become more powerful BusinessObjects users.

Some of the examples in this chapter require that the portfolio documents are exported into your repository. Many corporations, will not allow the use of external repositories, and/or non-corporate documents in the repository. Therefore, the examples that pertain to corporate documents or other repository functions, should be used as a guide, while you examine your own corporate documents and repository. Examples that open, save, or refresh documents can be completed without the use of a repository. For more information please contact us at rschmidt@schmidtink.com.

Starting the BusinessObjects Application

- The BusinessObjects application is not unlike any other application on your computer, at least not in the way it starts.
    - From the Start menu select
      Start->All Programs->Business Objects->BusinessObjects

    - The icon may also appear on your desktop as a shortcut

With most versions of BusinessObjects, there are at least two ways to open the BusinessObjects reporter.

- If there is a shortcut icon on the desktop, as shown above, simply double click it.
    - If a user wants to have a document open automatically or to have a script execute when the BusinessObjects application is opened a command line can be appended to the icon properties.
- BusinessObjects can also be started from the Start menu by accessing the BusinessObjects icon from the BusinessObjects group in the Programs group.

1. Click the Start button, located in the lower left corner of your monitor.
2. Click the All Programs entry in the Start menu.
3. Click the Business Objects folder within the All Programs menu.
4. Click the BusinessObjects 6.x application within the BusinessObjects folder.

9

Logging In

- To log in enter a user name and password into the two edit fields supplied. The User Name field will remember all successful names that have been entered on a machine.

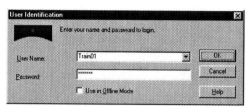

- If you try to log in three times unsuccessfully, you may be prohibited from logging in until you call your support desk.
- BusinessObjects can be logged into in offline mode by selecting the check box in the lower portion of the dialog.
    - Offline mode allows BusinessObjects to be logged into, even when when on an airplane! This allows you to format and analyze reports when there is no network to attach to.

Users must log into BusinessObjects. To log in, simply type your user name in the <u>User Name</u> field and your password in the <u>Password</u> field. If you have logged in previously, your user name may be selected by clicking on the down arrow associated with the User Name field.

If you are using a laptop computer that is not connected to the network, you may log in Offline. For example, you are on a bus or a plane. In this mode all documents can be reviewed or modified. This is very similar to reading your emails after they have been retrieved to your local machine.

Passwords usually are case-sensitive. This means that if your password contains capital letters, you must type them as capital letters when you log in. If you do not, it will be considered an unsuccessful attempt.

If you have a local installation, you may not be prompted to log in. This means that there is no security and no repository to store documents. In this mode, it works like most other Windows applications.

1. Enter your user name and password.
2. Click the OK button

10

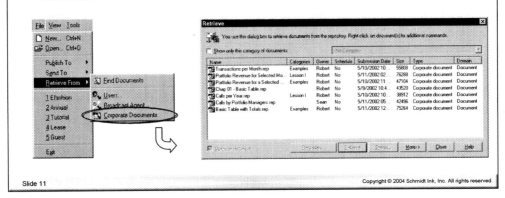

Retrieving Documents

- BusinessObjects stores some documents in a storage place called a repository. Documents in the repository can be created by you, other users in your group or a team responsible for creating documents.
- Documents are then retrieved from the repository and saved on your local drive. Then the documents can be opened and viewed.

The repository is a central location where documents are stored and shared. Documents can be placed in the repository through the following methods:

- They can be processed documents. These are documents that were scheduled for processing through the BusinessObjects Broadcast Server.
- They can be sent by other users. Users have the ability to send documents to other users.
- They can be placed in the corporate documents section for retrieval by many employees.

To retrieve a document, click on it to select it, and then click the <u>Retrieve</u> button. Multiple documents can be retrieved by holding down the [Ctrl] key while selecting them. If it is desired that the documents open upon retrieval, the <u>Open on Retrieval</u> option can be checked.

1. Select *File->Retrieve From->Corporate Documents...* from the menu.

11

Document Categories

- When documents are sent to the repository, they can be assigned a category. These categories help to identify the purpose of the document.

- Users can then filter the displayed documents by checking the <u>Show only this category of documents</u> option and selecting a category from the drop down list.

- To sort the documents by category, click the Categories header button.

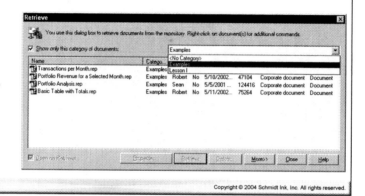

Since companies can have an overwhelming number of documents in their repository, BusinessObjects makes it possible to categorize the documents in the Retrieve dialog. There may be many categories, such as Month End Reports, Finance Reports, Marketing Reports and many more.

The documents can either be sorted or filtered by their categories. Sorting the categories displays the documents in the order of the categories and filtering the documents displays documents of only the selected category.

1. Sort the categories by clicking on the Categories header button in the document list.

2. Filter the categories by checking the Show only this category of documents option and choosing Examples from the drop down list.

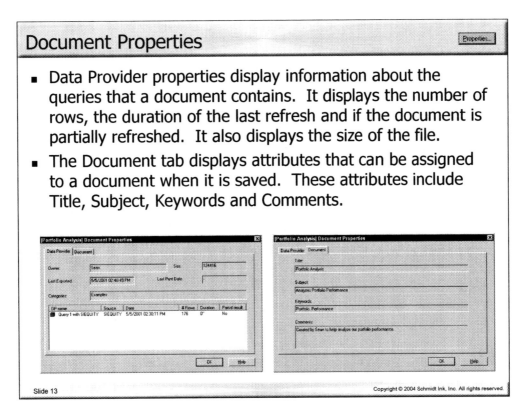

Document properties can be viewed by first selecting the document of interest in the Retrieve dialog and then clicking the Properties... button.

The Document Properties dialog contains two tabs - Data Provider and Document.

The Data Provider tab displays information about the data provider(s) contained in a document. Such as, the last refresh date, the number of rows returned, the duration of the last refresh and if it contains partial results or not. It also displays the size of the file. These attributes help users make important decisions, such as if they should download a large file and if the query duration is long, should they refresh the document.

The Document tab displays user assigned attributes that help identify the purpose of the document. These attributes can also help to locate documents, as will be seen in the following slide.

1. Select the Portfolio Analysis document in the list.
2. Click the *Properties...* button.

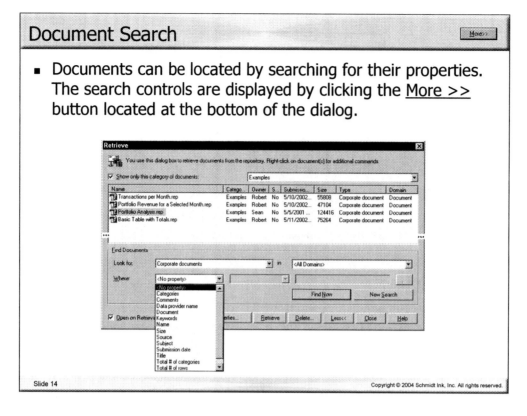

Documents are sometimes difficult to locate. Therefore, BusinessObjects has created an easy to use document search that helps you locate documents based on their attributes. The search will search by User, Processed, and Corporate documents.

1. Click the _More_ >> button in the Retrieve dialog.
2. Enter the following in the displayed fields
    - Look for: Corporate Documents.
    - In: <All Domains>.
    - Where: Title.
    - Contains: Analysis.
3. Make sure the _Show only this category of documents_ option is not checked.
4. Click the _Find Now_ button.
5. Retrieve the document by clicking on the _Retrieve_ button.

Opening Documents

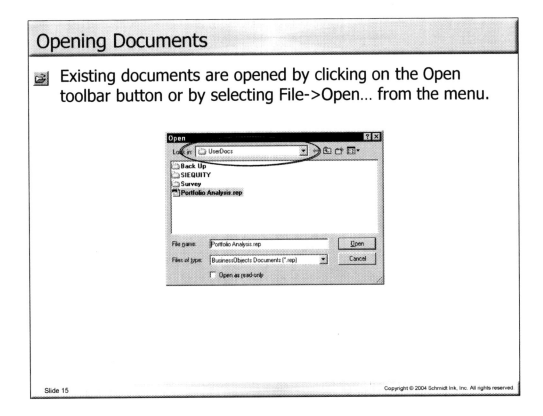

Existing documents are opened by clicking on the Open toolbar button or by selecting File->Open... from the menu.

Documents are opened with the Open dialog that is available to most Windows applications. To ensure that a document can not be changed, open it with the Open as Read Only option checked. If changes are made and it is desired to save the document, simply select File->Save As... from the menu and rename the document.

To open a document simply double-click on the desired document or click the Open button while the desired document(s) is (are) selected. To select multiple documents, hold down the [Ctrl] key while clicking on the desired documents.

1. Select *File->Open...* from the menu.
2. Select Portfolio Analysis.rep.
3. Click the Open button.

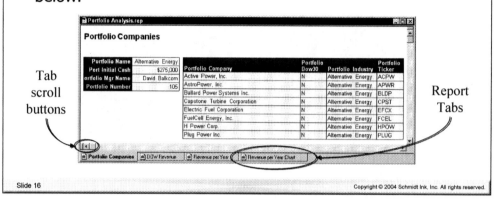

BusinessObjects allows several different types of report elements to be displayed in a report. These elements consist of blocks - Tables, cross tables and charts - and cells - cells contain information such as report titles, page numbers and dates.

These report elements are organized to form reports and a BusinessObjects document can contain many reports. Reports are identified in a document by the tabs along the bottom portion of a document. If there are many tabs, the tabs may all not be visible and if this happens, tab scroll buttons will appear in the lower left portion of the document.

1. Click on the Revenue per Year tab.
   This tab represents a report that has two tables – A rotated table and a crosstab.
2. Click on the Revenue per Year Chart tab
   Notice that the crosstab on the previous tab has been replaced with a chart.

All of the reports in this document are formatted using the Master-Detail format. This type of format works well when more than one table or report structure is needed to support a single statement. In this case the statement is the Portfolio.

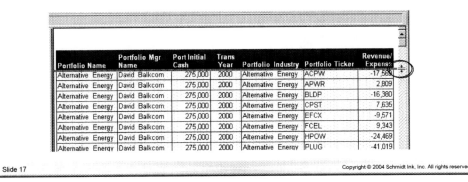

Splitting Report Windows

- You can split the viewable report into sections with their own scroll bars. This is often done for large reports where the user wants to view the headers at all times
- To split a window, click on the small rectangular thumb at the top or the left of the scroll bars and drag it to the desired location
    - Reports can also be split by selecting Window->Split from the menu.

Portfolio Name	Portfolio Mgr Name	Port Initial Cash	Trans Year	Portfolio Industry	Portfolio Ticker	Revenue/ Expense
Alternative Energy	David Balkcom	275,000	2000	Alternative Energy	ACPW	-17,56
Alternative Energy	David Balkcom	275,000	2000	Alternative Energy	APWR	2,809
Alternative Energy	David Balkcom	275,000	2000	Alternative Energy	BLDP	-16,380
Alternative Energy	David Balkcom	275,000	2000	Alternative Energy	CPST	7,635
Alternative Energy	David Balkcom	275,000	2000	Alternative Energy	EFCX	-9,571
Alternative Energy	David Balkcom	275,000	2000	Alternative Energy	FCEL	9,343
Alternative Energy	David Balkcom	275,000	2000	Alternative Energy	HPOW	-24,469
Alternative Energy	David Balkcom	275,000	2000	Alternative Energy	PLUG	-41,019

Often times we may want to split a report window. This allows us to hold one part of the report constant, while we scroll another part of the report. We often do this to hold the header portion of the report still, while we scroll the body of the report into it.

1. Click on the Portfolio List report tab.
2. Click on the small rectangular tab located above the vertical scroll bar and while holding the mouse button down, drag the tab to just beneath the table headings on the report.
3. Scroll the bottom half of the document so that the body of the report is scrolling into the header.

Duplicate/Delete a Report

- To duplicate a report within a document, select Edit->Duplicate Report from the menu
  - You may want to duplicate an existing report to
    - Modify existing formulas
    - Alter sorts and/or filters
    - Alter breaks
    - Summarize information
- To delete a report from a document, select Edit->Delete Report from the menu
  - You may want to delete a report from a document
    - Because it is no longer relevant
  - You cannot delete a report from a single report document

Documents Contain Data and Reports

- Documents store both data and reports. This allows the data that is stored within a document to be formatted many different ways within the same document.

- The data within a document is formatted to create reports. Refreshing the data will never change the format of a report.

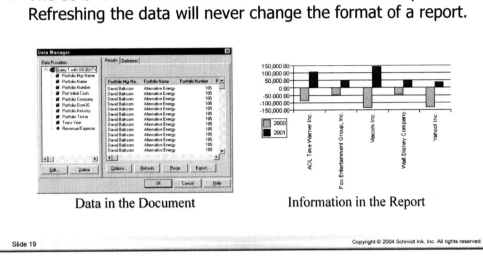

Data in the Document   Information in the Report

Since documents contain the data that the reports represent, the visible information can be displayed in many different fashions within a document.

Viewing Data and Statistics

- The data and query statistics in a document can be viewed by selecting Data->Edit... from the menu.
- The Results tab displays the data in a document.
- The Definition tab displays the dates and times in which a document has been refreshed. It also displays the number of rows returned and the duration of the refresh.

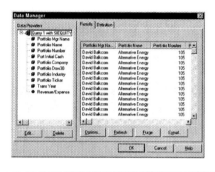 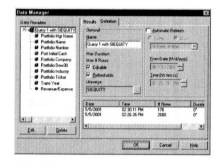

The Data Manager allows analysts to view the data contained within a document. It is sometimes necessary to view the data in this form to determine what the data looks like without the influence of report formats and formulas.

1. Select *Data->View...* from the menu.
2. Scroll down the data window on the Results tab.
3. Click on the Definition tab.
4. Observe the last Date and Time that this document was refreshed.
5. Observe how many rows were returned and the duration of the query.

20

Refreshing Documents

- After a document is opened, it can be refreshed using the Refresh toolbar button or by selecting Data->Refresh from the menu.

- Notice the status bar displays the number of rows being returned and the number of seconds the query is taking to refresh.

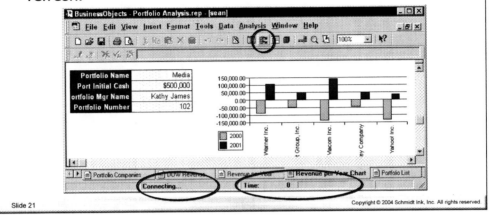

To refresh a document, simply click the Refresh toolbar button. Be aware that the time a query takes to refresh is highly dependent on the environment in which it exists. This means that a query can take anywhere from one second to several hours and more to refresh.

1. Select *Data->Refresh* from the menu.

21

- When a document is refreshed, BusinessObjects must create the instructions for the Data Warehouse and then send the instructions. The status bar reflects each of steps that BusinessObjects performs when refreshing a document
  - First it must analyze the query

    | Press Esc to Cancel | Analyzing... | Time: | 0 | 600 | |

  - Then it sends the query to the database to be executed

    | Press Esc to Cancel | | | |

  - Once the query has executed, the data is retrieved

    | Updating data... | Time: | 3 | 30 |

  - Then the data is formatted into a report

    | Report1: Computing data... | | |

  - Finally, the last execution date is displayed in the status bar

    | Last Exec: 3/7/98 04:36 PM | |

Some queries take so little time to complete that the steps barely have time to be displayed in the status bar. Other queries may take much longer and we find ourselves watching the status bar to follow the progress of our query.

Sometimes, a query may take so long that we may desire to cancel it by pressing the [ESC] button. However, this action will usually only cancel a query when it is in the Updating data phase.

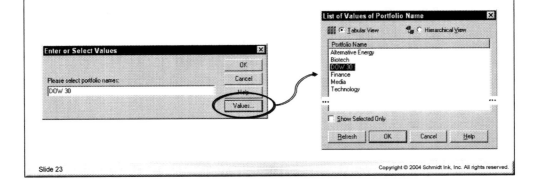

Entering Prompted Information

- When some documents are refreshed, a prompt dialog will be displayed. These dialogs request information that define the conditions placed on a document. For example, the box below is requesting the Year for which the document should get data for.
- To select values for the prompt, click the <u>Values...</u> button. Select values in the list and then click the OK button.

When a document displays a prompt dialog, the analyst must supply values to the supplied fields. You can have many prompt fields in the prompt dialog for on query. Moving your cursor into the various blank prompt areas and then clicking on the Values... button, will display a different list of values for each prompt.

Simply select your condition value(s) and then move your cursor to the next blank prompt area, then click on the Values... button again. Do this until all of the prompt fields contain at least one value.

Hitting the OK button will then cause your document to be refreshed with your selected condition values.

1. Retrieve Portfolio Analysis (prompted) from the Corporate Repository.
2. Click the Refresh button.
3. Click the Values... button in the prompt dialog.
4. Select DOW 30 from the pop-up dialog.
5. Click OK.

Refreshing the List of Values

- The values contained in the list of values dialog may not be updated each time the values button is clicked.
- The values for many lists are not volatile. For example, we rarely get a new country in the world.
- If you know that there are values that should appear in a list, click the Refresh button to update the list.

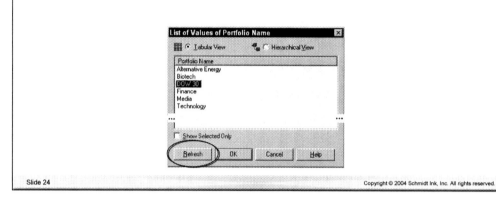

Refreshing the list of values, refreshes the values contained in the list with the most current information available. Once a list is refreshed, the values are saved on your computer. You will use this updated list each time you use the list of values for this object. When the list becomes obsolete again, simply click the Refresh button and again you will have an updated list.

Refreshing the list of values, does not refresh the document.

Tabular View Vs. Hierarchical View

- Tabular view lists the columns in a tabular fashion. With this view only the left-most column can be selected.
- Hierarchical view lists the right-most columns as folders, in very much the same manner as Windows Explorer. The folders can be browsed for values and when the desired value is found, it must be selected. BusinessObjects will ignore selected folders.

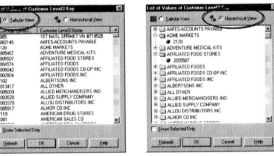

Tabular View   Hierarchical View

The tabular view is good for one or two column lists. The hierarchical view is good when there are multiple columns.

Some companies do not use multiple column lists for various reasons. Therefore, these companies, with single column lists, need not be concerned between the two views.

- Multiple list values can be selected in one of the follow ways
    - To select nonadjacent values, hold the [Ctrl] key down while selecting values.
    - To select adjacent values, first click on the uppermost value, then while holding down the [Shift] key, click on the lowermost value.
- When many nonadjacent values are selected, the <u>Show Selected Only</u> option can be checked to display only the selected values.

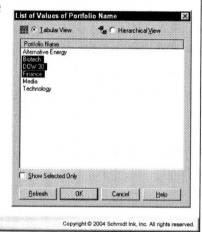

Any number of the values in the List of Values dialog can be selected. However, many databases can not handle a large number of values, so you should try not to select a large number of values. The term large varies from database to database and it also depends on the type of data being selected. For example, you could select more numerical values than textual values in some databases. A good rule of thumb is to try and keep the selected number below twenty or so values.

Tip

We often open reports that were refreshed by other users and we are not sure which values they selected when they last refreshed the document. To easily inspect the selected values, click in the edit field on the prompt dialog and click the Values... button. Then check the Show Selected Only option. This will allow you to view only the values that were selected during the last refresh.

Saving Documents

🖫 Documents are saved by clicking the Save toolbar button or by selecting File->Save or File->Save As... from the menu.

■ Documents can be saved in a variety of formats, by selecting a type from the Save as type: combo box.

■ The Save for all users option allows documents to be saved without any security. This means that anyone with BusinessObjects on their computer can open the document.

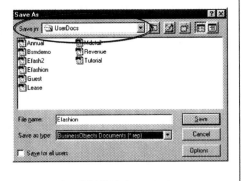

Users often save documents in the
..\My Documents\ My Business Objects Documents\UserDocs\ directory, which is the default directory. This is convenient because the documents are easy to locate and open.

BusinessObjects Document (*.rep): A standard document that can be shared with others users who own BusinessObjects.

Rich Text Format (*.rtf): Saves the document as Rich Text, which many word processors can open.

Text (.txt): Save the document as text. Much of a report's format is lost.

Portable Document Format (*.pdf): Saves document as an Acrobat file. This format is very portable.

Microsoft Excel Worksheet (*.xls): Creates an Excel file that can be shared with others that have MS Excel.

HTML (*.htm): Saves the document in a format that is compatible with most WEB browsers.

BusinessObjects Template (*.ret): This saves the general format of a document, which can be used to format other documents.

BusinessQuery files (*.bqy): This saves only the query and data in a document.

BusinessObjects Addins (*.rea): Saves the VBA in a document.

- Documents can be saved every x minutes, using the Automatic Save option.
- Documents can be set to refresh upon opening, using the Refresh Document When Opening option.
- An open password or a Write Reserve password can also be assigned.

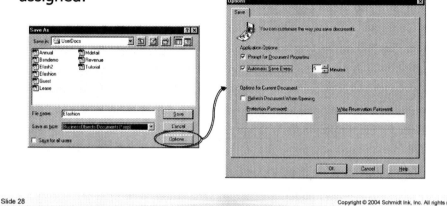

BusinessObjects allows several options to be assigned to documents. These options include the following.

Automatic Save Every x Minutes

This option is often used when creating complicated documents. If this option is used, then the document is only as old as the last save.

Refresh Document When Opening

This option causes the document to be refreshed when it is opened. If this option is set, the document will always display the current data when the document is opened. While this is a good option, it probably should not be used on documents that take a relatively long time to refresh.

Protection Password

If a value is assigned to this field, the document can not be opened unless the value is reentered upon opening.

Write Reservation Password

If a value is assigned to this field, the document can not be saved unless the value is reentered upon opening.

Saving Documents - Properties

- When a document is saved, it will prompt for the document properties, if the Prompt for Document Properties option is checked.
- Properties help users search for documents in the Repository and also help documents to be identified.

The properties of a document help to identify the document and its purposes. The properties can be viewed when retrieving documents from the Corporate Documents, Other users or the Broadcast Agent.

Some of the properties are not editable by the user, such as its location, its creation date, its modification date and the date it was last printed.

However, some of the properties are user definable, such as the documents Title, Subject, Author, Keywords and comments.

1. Select *File->Save As...* from the menu.
2. Click the *Options* button in the Save As dialog.
3. Check the Prompt for Document Properties option in the Option dialog.
4. Click the OK button in the Options dialog.
5. Enter a new document name in the Save As dialog and click OK.
6. Modify the current document properties.

29

Sharing Documents with Specific Users

- Documents can be shared with other users by selecting File->Send To->Users... from the menu.
- To select which users to send to, click the To... button for a list of available users and groups.

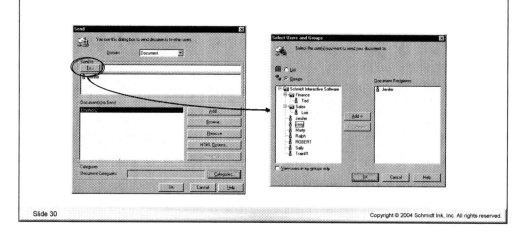

T he Send dialog opens with the current document ready to send. To add additional opened documents, click the Add... button. To add unopened documents click the Browse... button. If you want to send an HTML version of the document, mainly for Web Intelligence users, click the HTML options button and assign the document HTML features. To schedule the send using the Broadcast Agent, click the Schedule... button.

The document can be assigned a category for easy identification by clicking on the Categories... button.

Documents can be retrieved from other users by first selecting File->Retrieve From->Users... and then selecting the documents in the Retrieve dialog.

1. Select *File->Send To->Users...*
2. Click the To... button and select yourself from the list of users.
3. Click the OK button.
4. Click the OK button.

Publishing Corporate Documents

- With BusinessObjects, documents can be published to the Corporate Documents.

- Publishing documents differs from sending to users, because the documents are available to all users in a group. Also when documents are retrieved, they are not removed from the Repository.

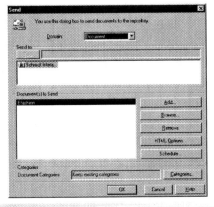

The Corporate Documents is a place where documents can be shared with all users in a group. These documents will stay in the Cooperate Document space until they are deleted.

31

First Level Course for BusinessObjects Reporter

Report Structures

Introduction

- In order to effectively present information in reports, it is important to understand how to create and manipulate the different report structures available in BusinessObjects. In this chapter, we are going to
    - Learn about the different data objects available
    - Discuss freestanding cells
        - Inserting, copying, moving, formatting
    - Explore tables
        - Applying calculations and breaks, rotating moving, copying, and inserting and deleting columns
    - Discover crosstabs
        - Inserting, converting tables, applying aggregate functions, calculating the variance between two columns, and inserting breaks
    - Examine charts
        - Inserting charts, converting tables to charts, Moving and sizing, and multiple measures

Data Types

- All report structures contain some sort of information. This information can be a report title, employee ID, department, sales revenue, number of transactions, and so forth
- BusinessObjects allows for four different types of information
  - Text
    - Any literal entered directly into a report, such as titles and labels
  - Dimension
    - Uniquely identifies factors in a report. Dimensions are usually nouns, such as employee id, date, transaction number, department, ...
  - Detail
    - Usually support a dimension. Details usually have a one-to-one relationship with dimensions. Details can be phone numbers, employee name, product description, and so forth
  - Measure
    - Quantitative information that conforms to the dimensions and details in a report, such as a sum of salaries or a count of transactions

It is important to understand how the different objects behave in a report. This allows us to anticipate how our reports will calculate. It also gives us the ability to create more complex reports by taking advantage of each object's qualities.

Cells

- All reports contain cells in one form or another
    - Titles, run dates, and, header and footer notes are often contained in freestanding cells.
        - Freestanding cells are cells that are not associated with a report block, such as a table, crosstab, or a chart.
    - Tables and crosstabs are formed with cells that are arranged to form columns and rows.
    - The axis labels, titles, and values in charts are displayed in cells.

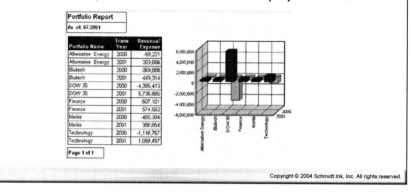

Every report has cells – either freestanding or in report structures. In these next few slides we will discuss various aspects of cells.

Formatting Cells

- Cells can be formatted with the Cell Format dialog
  - To format a freestanding cell or a cell in a table or crosstab, right-click on the cell and select *Format Cell...* from the pop-up menu. You may also select *Format>Cell...* from the main menu.
  - To format an axis label, right-click on the label and select Format Axis Label... from the pop-up menu. You may also select *Format>Axis Label...* from the main menu.

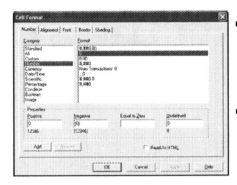

- The Cell format dialog contains five tabs (four tabs for axis labels) that allow you to apply various formats to selected cells.
- There are usually several format fields that represent the different states of the cell's value.

The Format Cell dialog allows us to format cells in many ways. We can format the contents of the cell and the cell itself. We can hide freestanding cells, shade cells, format the border, format the font, control the alignment, and format the physical appearance of the data in the cell.

1. Open Ex 02 01.rep.
2. Click on any cell in the report.
3. Select *Format>Cell...* from the menu.
4. Browse through the tabs and become familiar with their functionality.

37

Formatting Header Cells

- Header cells can contain long descriptions of the columns below them. This causes reports to be wider than necessary, which limits the number of columns that will fit on a page.
  - The Alignment tab will allow you to Wrap Text. This will enable long descriptions to wrap in a cell.
    - You will have to make the cell taller to accommodate the extra lines. It is also a good idea to bottom align all header cells.

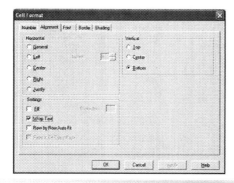

This is a good practice, since the headers are often wider than the contents of the cells. This practice will allow you to fit more information in a report.

1. Open Ex 02 01.rep.
2. Click on the Format Header report tab.
3. Select each of the blue header cells by holding down the [Ctrl] key and clicking on each of them.
4. Select *Format>Cell...* from the menu.
5. Click on the Alignment tab to activate it.
6. Select Wrap Text in the Settings section.
7. Select Bottom in the Vertical section.
8. Click OK.
9. Double-click the bottom border of the header cells. This will cause it to resize to display multiple lines.

Standard Cell Format

- BusinessObjects allows you to preformat freestanding cells, using the Standard Report Styles dialog.
  - Select Tools>Standard Report Styles... from the menu.
  - This dialog allows you to set the formats to company standards, so you do not have to reformat the default format.

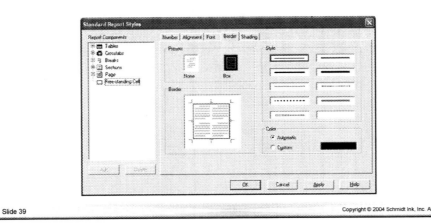

Since different companies have different format standards, Business Objects allows you to set the formats of cells before they are even created. This allows your company or department to have report standards that are easy to adhere to.

39

Moving/Copying/Sizing Cells

- **To move a cell**
  - Click anywhere on the cell to select it. Then, click on it again and hold the mouse button down. Move the cell to a new location and release the mouse button. (If you hold the [CTRL] the cell will be copied to the new location.)

- **To copy a cell**
  - Click anywhere on the cell to select it. Then select *Edit>Copy* from the menu. Click anywhere on the report to place the upper-left corner of the cell and select Edit>Paste from the menu.

- **To size a cell**
  - Place the cursor over the left or bottom edge. The cursor will change to the size cursor. Then click and drag the edge out to a new width or height.

    Page 1 of 1

You can move any cell on a report, even the ones in a table. This functionality gives us many formatting options.

1. Click on the header cell of the report.

2. Let go of the mouse button and click on it again. This time hold the mouse button down. Now you can drag the cell around the report.

3. Hold down the [Ctrl] key and look at the drag cursor. It now has a plus (+) appended to it. This plus means that it will now copy the cell.

4. Let the mouse button go to move or copy the cell.

5. Place your cursor at the right-edge of the header cell. Notice that it changes form to a sizing cursor.

6. Click and drag the cell to a new size.

Inserting Cells

- To insert a cell into a report
  - Click the *Insert Cell* toolbar button and then place the upper-right corner of the cell by clicking on the report

- To insert an identical cell under or beside an existing cell
  - Select the cell, then click one of the insert cell toolbar buttons

- After a cell has been inserted
  - Text may be entered directly into the cell
  - An object from the Report Manager may be placed in the cell.

We insert cells into reports for many reasons. We insert freestanding cells for run dates, page numbers, displaying prompts, summaries, and so forth. We also insert cells into tables for calculations, data from other sources, and so forth.

1. Click on the title cell to select it.
2. Click the Insert Cell Below toolbar button.
3. Double-click on the newly inserted cell and type Portfolio Revenue by Date.
4. Press the [Return] key.
5. Click the Center toolbar button, to center the new text.

41

- There are two methods of inserting graphics into a report
  - Select *Insert>Picture...* from the menu. Click on the report to place the upper-left corner of the graphic. Select the file in the open dialog.
    - This method will insert a graphic into a report, but the aspect ratio of the graphic is not preserved. This means that the picture may be distorted. In addition, the file must seem to be in the same location to every viewer of the report.
  - Select *Insert>Object...* from the menu. Click on the report to place the upper-left corner of the object. Select Create from File in the Insert Object dialog. Locate the file and click OK.
    - This method is better, because it embeds the graphic into the document. It also preserves it's aspect ratio.

  - If you inserted a picture, and then the file was later deleted, then BusinessObjects would replace the picture with the graphic to the left.

Many times, we want to insert a graphic into our reports. In many cases this graphic is our company logo.

1. Select *Insert>Object...* from the menu.
2. Click anywhere on the report, where you want to place a graphic.
3. Select the Create From File option in the Insert Object dialog.
4. Click the Browse... button to locate the file (SurfPhoto.bmp).
5. Select the file and click OK.
6. Click OK again, if needed.

Tables

- **Tables consist of rows of information**
  - Each row is defined by a unique combination of the dimension and detail values, which means that there should be no two rows in a table that are identical
  - If a table contains a measure, it will conform to the rows of the table.
    - Each measure usually has a default aggregate function assigned to it. This causes them to always sum, average, min, max, or count to conform to the dimension defined rows.
- **Most tables have a header row**
  - Header rows are not defined by combinations of dimensions
  - Header rows are singular in nature
  - Header rows typically contain labels for the columns of the table

Portfolio Name	Trans Year	Revenue/Expense
Alternative Energy	2000	-89,221.30
Alternative Energy	2001	303,885.90
Biotech	2000	-369,888.40
Biotech	2001	449,314.10
DOW 30	2000	-4,385,412.50
DOW 30	2001	5,736,865.50
Finance	2000	-507,100.70
Finance	2001	574,563.00
Media	2000	-465,393.90
Media	2001	386,853.60
Technology	2000	-1,116,767.25
Technology	2001	1,059,497.45

Almost all reports start out as a table. Once created, tables can be transformed into charts, crosstabs, and rotated tables.

1. Open Ex 02 02.rep.

Table Headers and Footers

- Table headers allow us to insert column labels. Table footers allow us to insert summary calculations that operate on the data in the column above it (Technically, they operate on the context defined by the footer, but this is an advanced topic).
- Use the Show Header / Show Footer options in the Table Format dialog to show or hide the footers.
  - Click on the table and then select *Format>Table...* from the menu to display the Table Format dialog
  - Notice that you can also Fold a table. This option allows the rows of a table to be hidden. Thus only displaying the header and footer of the table.

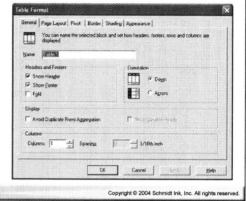

Table headers and footers allow you to insert summary information into a table. They also allow us to identify the columns.

1. Click on the table and select *Format>Table...* from the menu.
2. Click on the General tab to activate it.
3. Select the Show Footer option in the Headers and Footers section of the dialog.
4. Click Ok.

Standard Table Format

- The Standard Report Styles dialog allows you to preformat the header, body, and footer of tables in all of your documents, before they are created.
  - Select *Tools>Standard Report Styles...*
  - The dialog below, sets the standard for table headers to the standard suggested in the previous slide.

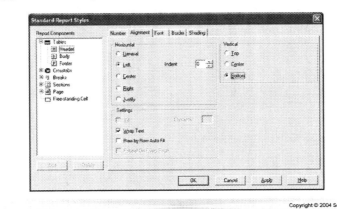

Since different companies have different format standards, Business Objects allows you to set the formats of tables before they are even created. This allows your company or department to have report standards that are easy to adhere to.

If you have used BusinessObjects 5.x and 6.x, you should notice that in version 5.x the body of a table is yellow. In 6.x, the default for the body is white.

1. Select *Tools>Standard Report Styles...* from the menu.
2. Expand the Tables option, by clicking on the plus (+) sign preceding it.
3. Select the Header option within the Table class.
4. Click on the Alignment tab to activate it.
5. Select Wrap Text from the Settings section.
6. Select Bottom in the Vertical section.

This is the default format that is use throughout most of this book.

Applying Calculations to a Column

- To apply a calculation to a column
  - Select any value in the column
  - Select Data->Calculations->*
    - Where * can be Sum, Count, Count All, Average, Minimum, Maximum, Percentage, Variance, or Variance Percentage
- Calculations apply to all visible values in the column
- Calculations add a footer row to the table

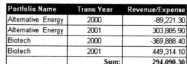

Portfolio Name	Trans Year	Revenue/Expense
Alternative Energy	2000	-89,221.30
Alternative Energy	2001	303,885.90
Biotech	2000	-369,888.40
Biotech	2001	449,314.10

Σ

Portfolio Name	Trans Year	Revenue/Expense
Alternative Energy	2000	-89,221.30
Alternative Energy	2001	303,885.90
Biotech	2000	-369,888.40
Biotech	2001	449,314.10
	Sum:	294,090.30

When a calculation is applied to a column, the result is displayed in the footer. These types of calculations aggregate the data in the column.

In applications, like MS Excel, the calculations actually use the values in the cells on the report. However, in BusinessObjects, the calculations in the footer are independent of the values in the column. The calculations in BusinessObjects actually aggregate the information in the document (micro-cube or dataset) and then display the results in the footer. We will learn more about this later in the class.

This example will insert a sum and an average into the footer of a table.

1. Select any revenue value in the Revenue/Expense column.
2. Click the Insert Sum toolbar button.
3. Select *Data>Calculations>Average*.

Applying a Break to a Table

- To apply a break to a table
  - Select a value in any dimension column
  - Select Insert->Break from the menu
- A break will
  - Insert a footer row each time the value in the break column changes
  - Insert a footer at the end of the table
  - Not add any calculations to the table
- A break groups the values in the break column
- A break allows subtotals to be inserted into a table

Portfolio Name	Trans Year	Revenue/Expense
Alternative Energy	2000	-89,221.30
Alternative Energy	2001	303,885.90
Biotech	2000	-369,888.40
Biotech	2001	449,314.10
	Sum:	294,090.30

Portfolio Name	Trans Year	Revenue/Expense
Alternative Energy	2000	-89,221.30
	2001	303,885.90
Alternative Energy	Sum:	214,664.60
Biotech	2000	-369,888.40
	2001	449,314.10
Biotech	Sum:	79,425.70
	Sum:	294,090.30

Breaks allow us to separate data into groups based on the values of one or more dimensions. We can then place subtotals and other summary information in the footers of these groups.

1. Click on any Portfolio Name in the Portfolio Name column.
2. Click the Insert Break toolbar button.
3. Click on any revenue in the Revenue/Expense column.
4. Click the Insert Sum button (You may have to click it twice, if the sum has already been applied).
5. Select *Data>Calculations>Average*.

Notice that when the break was applied to the Portfolio Name column, the footers did not automatically contain the sums and averages that we applied in the previous example. This is because BusinessObjects cannot assume that the calculations are also needed at the break level summaries.

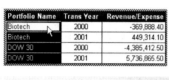
Rotating tables gives us another way to present information in a tabular form. It usually works best with tables that have few rows of information.

These types of rotated tables are often referred to as records, because they work best with sets of information. For example, a student record that may consist of Name, Address, Phone Number, Class Level, Dorm Room, and so forth.

1. Click on the Table to Rotate tab to activate that report.
2. Click anywhere on the table to select it.
3. Click on the Rotate Table toolbar button.

Breaks and Rotated Tables

- We can place a break in a rotated table so that a side-by-side comparison can be achieved.
- To place the break, select a dimension in the table, and then select Insert->Break from the menu.
  - To place the sums, select a measure value and select Data->Calculations->Sum from the menu.

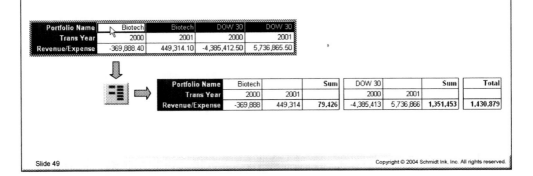

Portfolio Name	Biotech	Biotech	DOW 30	DOW 30
Trans Year	2000	2001	2000	2001
Revenue/Expense	-369,888.40	449,314.10	-4,385,412.50	5,736,865.50

Portfolio Name	Biotech		Sum	DOW 30		Sum	Total
Trans Year	2000	2001		2000	2001		
Revenue/Expense	-369,888	449,314	79,426	-4,385,413	5,736,866	1,351,453	1,430,879

Breaks in rotated tables allow us to group the different records in a table by dimension values. This is probably only useful with rotated tables that have few dimension values, since if there are too many, it may span right off the right-side of the page.

1. Click on any portfolio name in the Portfolio Name column.
2. Click the Insert Break toolbar button.
3. Click on any revenue in the Revenue/Expense row and click the Insert Sum toolbar button.

- **To move a table**
  - Click on the edge of the table, hold the mouse button down, and drag the table to a new location
  - The cursor will turn to a four way directional cross, when over the edge of the report
- **To copy a table**
  - Do the same as the move section above, but hold down the [Ctrl] key before releasing the mouse button
  - Click on the edge of the table, select Edit->Copy, click on the report where the table is to go, and then select Edit->Paste

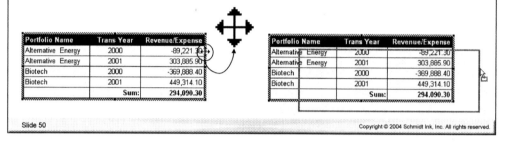

Portfolio Name	Trans Year	Revenue/Expense
Alternative Energy	2000	-89,221.70
Alternative Energy	2001	303,885.90
Biotech	2000	-369,888.40
Biotech	2001	449,314.10
	Sum:	294,090.30

Portfolio Name	Trans Year	Revenue/Expense
Alternative Energy	2000	-89,221.30
Alternative Energy	2001	303,885.90
Biotech	2000	-369,888.40
Biotech	2001	449,314.10
	Sum:	294,090.30

Since tables can be transformed into any other report structure, we often copy tables to other locations on a report. Then, we transform them into other report components.

Move a Table

1. Click on the Table to Move report tab to activate that report.
2. Move your cursor over the edge of the table.
3. When your cursor turns into the move cursor, click and drag the table to a new location.

Copy a Table

1. Move your cursor over the edge of the table.
2. When your cursor turns into the move cursor, click and drag the table to a new location.
3. Before releasing the mouse button, hold down the [Ctrl] button. Notice the plus (+) sign appended to the cursor.

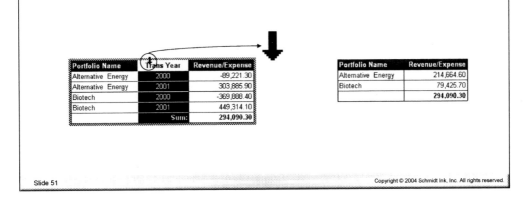

Deleting a Column From a Table

- To delete a column from a table
  - Place the cursor over the top edge of the top cell. The cursor will turn to an arrow
  - Select Edit->Delete from the menu
- If you delete a dimension column, the measure column will accurately conform to the new combination of dimensions

When deleting a column, it is important to select the entire column, so you do not partially delete it. For example, you can actually just delete a header cell and leave the column beneath it intact.

Delete a Column

1. Move your cursor to the top of the Trans Year Column and move it down, until the cursor changes into a down arrow cursor.
2. Click to select the entire column.
3. Right-click on the selection and choose Delete from the pop-up menu.

51

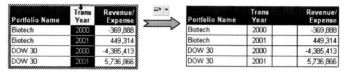
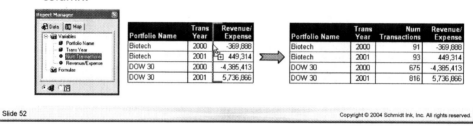
When inserting a column into a table using the drag and drop method, be sure that the column is only partially selected before dropping the object into the report. If the column is fully selected, then the object will replace the column.

1. Drag the Trans Year object from the Report Manager. If the Report Manager is not visible, then select *View>Report Manager* from the menu to show it.

2. Drag the Trans Year object to the right side of the Portfolio Name column or the left side of the Revenue/Expense column.

3. When the selection is only on half the column, drop the Trans Year object.

52

Hiding Columns

- We may want to hide a column in a table, because it is necessary to the table's configuration, but not necessary to display.
    - We may want to hide a column that is used to define a sort.
    - We may want to hide a column that is necessary for a calculation.
- To hide a column
    - Right-click on a table and select Format table...
    - Activate the Pivot tab.
    - Select the object to hide.
    - Click the hide button.

Many reports have hidden columns that allow a table to behave in a desired way. However, as people become more skilled at BusinessObjects, the need for these hidden columns begins to diminish. So as your skills begin to increase, you should go back and revisit some report that have hidden columns and reevaluate if these hidden columns are actually necessary.

1. Click on any value in the table.
2. Select *Format>Table...* from the menu.
3. Click on the Pivot tab to activate it.
4. Click on the Trans Year object in the Used Variables section.
5. Click the Hide button.
6. Click OK.

- **Crosstabs are special summary tables that have**
  - Dimensions for column and row headers
  - Measure summaries in the body
- **Crosstabs create intersections between two dimensions, where measures can aggregate for the two dimension values**
  - For example, for the dimension values Alternative Energy and 2000, the measure value is −89,221.30

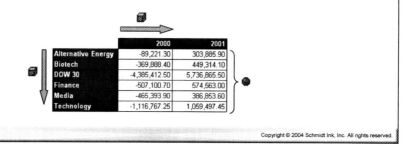

	2000	2001
Alternative Energy	-89,221.30	303,885.90
Biotech	-369,888.40	449,314.10
DOW 30	-4,385,412.50	5,736,865.50
Finance	-507,100.70	574,563.00
Media	-465,393.90	386,853.60
Technology	-1,116,767.25	1,059,497.45

Crosstabs are probably the most common report structure, because they supply a lot of information in a relatively compact package and they are easy to understand. As you become more skillful, you will learn that there are many ways that you can format crosstabs to provide even more information.

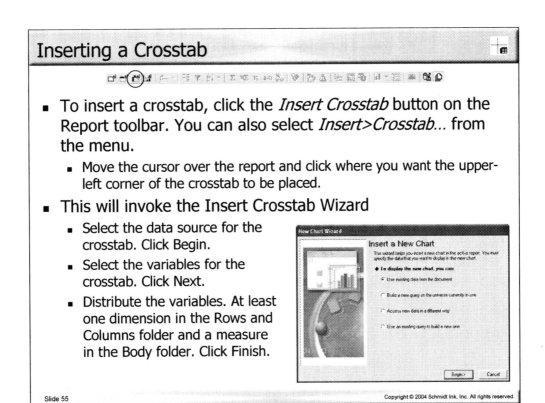

Inserting a Crosstab

- To insert a crosstab, click the *Insert Crosstab* button on the Report toolbar. You can also select *Insert>Crosstab...* from the menu.
  - Move the cursor over the report and click where you want the upper-left corner of the crosstab to be placed.
- This will invoke the Insert Crosstab Wizard
  - Select the data source for the crosstab. Click Begin.
  - Select the variables for the crosstab. Click Next.
  - Distribute the variables. At least one dimension in the Rows and Columns folder and a measure in the Body folder. Click Finish.

Most of the time, we convert tables to crosstabs, but once in a while we will insert one directly. Therefore, we will start with inserting one into our sample report.

1. Open Ex 02 03.rep
2. Select *Insert>Crosstab...* from the menu.
3. Click on the Insert report tab to activate the report.
4. Move your cursor over the blank report and click where the upper-left corner of the crosstab will be placed.
5. Select *Use existing data from the document*. This option allows us to insert a crosstab with the data that is currently in the document.
6. Click Begin>.
7. Select two dimensions (Portfolio Name and Trans Year) and the measure (Revenue/Expense).
8. Click Next>.
9. Make sure that Portfolio Name is in the Columns folder, Trans Year is in the Rows folder and Revenue/Expense is in the Body folder.
10. Click Finish>.

Standard Crosstab Format

- The Standard Report Styles dialog allows you to preformat the headers, body, footers, and corners of crosstabs in all of your new documents.
  - Select *Tools>Standard Report Styles...*
  - Since crosstabs have headers on the top and left, and footers on the bottom and right, we can format the different orientations.

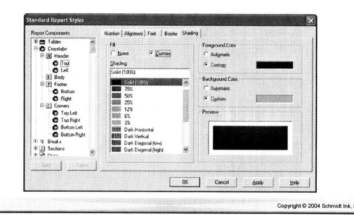

Since different companies have different format standards, Business Objects allows you to set the formats of tables before they are even created. This allows your company or department to have report standards that are easy to adhere to.

If you have used BusinessObjects 5.x and 6.x, you should notice that in version 5.x the body of a table was yellow. In 6.x, the default for the body is white.

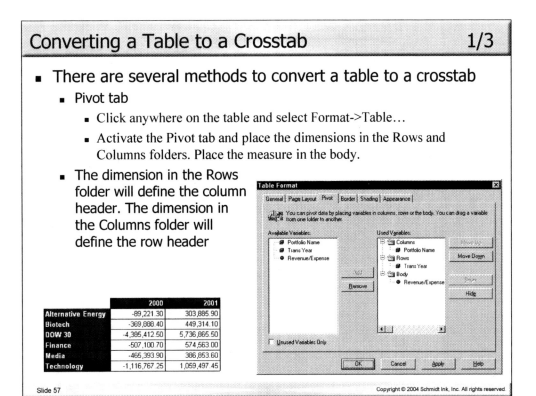

- There are several methods to convert a table to a crosstab
  - Pivot tab
    - Click anywhere on the table and select Format->Table…
    - Activate the Pivot tab and place the dimensions in the Rows and Columns folders. Place the measure in the body.
  - The dimension in the Rows folder will define the column header. The dimension in the Columns folder will define the row header

	2000	2001
Alternative Energy	-89,221.30	303,885.90
Biotech	-369,888.40	449,314.10
DOW 30	-4,385,412.50	5,736,865.50
Finance	-507,100.70	574,563.00
Media	-465,393.90	386,853.60
Technology	-1,116,767.25	1,059,497.45

It is a good idea to convert the default report table to a crosstab, because this method allows you to modify the table by adding and deleting columns, before creating the crosstab.

1. Click on the Format Table – Pivot Tab report tab to activate it.
2. Click anywhere on the table.
3. Select *Format>Table…* from the menu.
4. Click on the Pivot tab to activate it.
5. In the Used Variables section
   - Drag Portfolio Name to the Columns folder.
   - Drag Trans Year to the Rows folder
   - Leave Revenue/Expense in the Body folder.
6. Click OK.

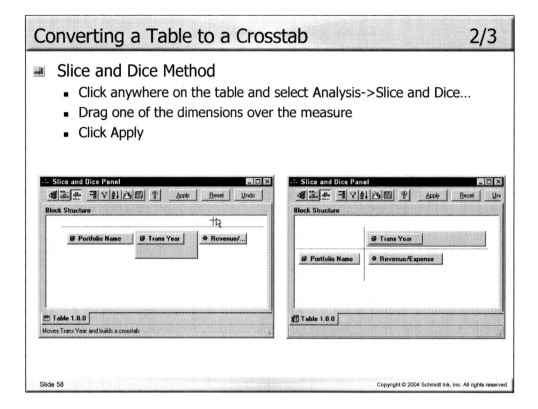

Many new users like to use the Slice and Dice Panel. It is a powerful tool that allows you to quickly see the structure and many attributes of your report. That being said, it is important to know that the panel can be misleading at times. For example, it does not display global filters, hidden sorts, or footer calculations.

1. Click on the Slice and Dice report tab to activate it.
2. Click anywhere on the table.
3. Select *Analysis>Slice and Dice...* from the menu
4. Drag the Trans Year object above the dashed line and above the Revenue/Expense object.
5. Click Apply.
6. Click the **x** in the upper-right corner of the panel to dismiss the dialog.

- Drag and Drop Method
  - Click on any dimension value in the table
  - Click on it again and drag it to the uppermost part of the leftmost header cell
  - Release the mouse button when the cursor changes to the crosstab

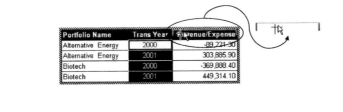

Portfolio Name	Trans Year	Revenue/Expense
Alternative Energy	2000	-89,221.30
Alternative Energy	2001	303,885.90
Biotech	2000	-369,888.40
Biotech	2001	449,314.10

This is perhaps the most convenient method to create a crosstab. However, it may take a little practice.

1. Click on any value in the Trans Year column.
2. Click on the same value again and this time hold down the button.
3. Drag the cell to the upper part of the Revenue/Expense header.
4. When the cursor turns into a crosstab cursor, release the mouse button.

If you did everything correct, you will have a crosstab. If you did not, you may have a master detail report or a #multivalue in the header cell. Click the undo button and try again. Becoming proficient using this method will greatly increase your BusinessObjects productivity.

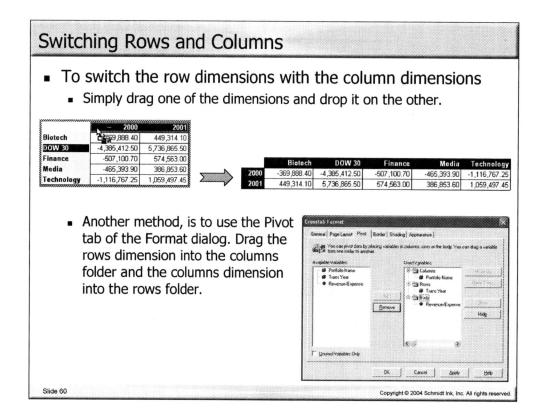

BusinessObjects has many features that make OLAP effortless. For example, if you drag a cell onto an existing cell, the contents of the cells will swap. This allows you to quickly switch the row and column headers of a crosstab.

Another method of switching the row and column headers, is to use the Slice and Dice panel. This is done by rearranging the objects in the panel.

Switch Rows and Columns Using Drag and Drop

1. Click on any value in the Portfolio Name column.

2. Click on it again, and this time drag it to the Trans Year row.

3. Drop it on any Trans Year value and the Rows will swap with the Columns.

Slice and Dice Method

1. Click on the Slice and Dice toolbar button.

2. Click on the Portfolio Name object in the Block Structure window.

3. Drag it to directly on top of the Trans Year object in the structure.

4. Before releasing the mouse button, press the [Shift] key.

5. The objects will trade places.

Applying Aggregate Calculations to a Crosstab

- To apply an aggregate calculation to a crosstab
  - Select any measure value in the body
  - Select Data->Calculations->*
- The calculation will place two footers on the crosstab
  - Horizontal footer will aggregate the values in the columns
  - Vertical footer will aggregate the values in the rows
  - The intersection of these two footers is the grand total cell

	2000	2001
Alternative Energy	-89,221	303,886
Biotech	-369,888	449,314
DOW 30	-4,385,413	5,736,866
Finance	-507,101	574,563
Media	-465,394	386,854
Technology	-1,116,767	1,059,497

	2000	2001	Sum:
Alternative Energy	-89,221	303,886	214,665
Biotech	-369,888	449,314	79,426
DOW 30	-4,385,413	5,736,866	1,351,453
Finance	-507,101	574,563	67,462
Media	-465,394	386,854	-78,540
Technology	-1,116,767	1,059,497	-57,270
Sum:	-6,933,784	8,510,980	1,577,196

Aggregate calculations in a crosstab aggregate the measures across and down. This is very useful, because we can see summaries for two different sets of dimensions.

1. Click on any value in the body of the cross tab (Revenue/Expense).
2. Click the Insert Sum toolbar button.
3. Click on any value in the body of the cross tab (Revenue/Expense).
4. Select *Data>Calculations>Average* from the menu.

61

Calculating the Variance of Two Columns

- To calculate the variance of two columns
    - Click on the header of the first column in the calculation
    - Hold down the [Ctrl] key and click on the second header
    - Select either
        - Data->Calculations->Variance
        - Data->Calculations->Variance Percentage
- The variance calculation allows you to calculate the difference and the percent difference between two columns

	2000	2001	2001-2000
Alternative Energy	78	96	18
Biotech	91	93	2
DOW 30	675	816	141
Finance	45	75	30
Media	62	58	-4
Technology	274	317	43

	2000	2001	2001-2000
Alternative Energy	78	96	23.08 %
Biotech	91	93	2.20 %
DOW 30	675	816	20.89 %
Finance	45	75	66.67 %
Media	62	58	-6.45 %
Technology	274	317	15.69 %

In most reporting tools, columns in crosstabs can only aggregate, which means they can sum, average, count, min, etc. However, BusinessObjects allows us to determine the difference between two columns.

Variance (Columns)

1. Click the Crosstab Variance report tab to activate it.
2. Click on the 2001 value in the crosstab header.
3. Hold down the [Ctrl] key and click the year 2000.
4. Click the Insert Variance toolbar button.

Percent Variance (Rows)

1. Click on the DOW 30 value in the left edge of the crosstab.
2. Hold down the [Ctrl] key and select Finance.
3. Click the Insert Variance Percentage toolbar button.

Applying a Break to a Crosstab

- Since Crosstabs have dimensions in both the column headers and the row headers, we can place a break on either
  - To place the break, click on any dimension value
  - Select Insert->Break
- Reapply calculations to populate the break footers

Year	Qtr	Biotech	DOW 30	Sum:
2000	3	43	322	365
	4	48	353	401
2000		91	675	766
2001	1	37	369	406
	2	45	372	417
	3	11	75	86
2001		93	816	909
	Sum:	184	1,491	1,675

| Year | Qtr | 2000 | | 2000 | 2001 | | | 2001 | Sum: |
		3	4		1	2	3		
Biotech		43	48	91	37	45	11	93	184
DOW 30		322	353	675	369	372	75	816	1,491
	Sum:	365	401	766	406	417	86	909	1,675

Breaks make almost any multi-dimension report more interesting, because they allow us to group dimension values and insert summary calculations.

Vertical Break

1. Click on the Apply a Break report tab to activate it.
2. Click on any year value in the top crosstab.
3. Click the Insert Break toolbar button.
4. Click on any Revenue/Expense value in the body.
5. Click the Insert Sum toolbar button.

Horizontal Break

1. Click on any year value in the lower table.
2. Click the Insert Break toolbar button.
3. Click on any Revenue/Expense value in the body.
4. Click the Insert Sum toolbar button.

Charts

- Charts allow us to graphically display information. They are typically used to compare the magnitudes of measures for different dimension values.
- Usually dimensions populate the X and Z axes, and measures populate the Y axis.

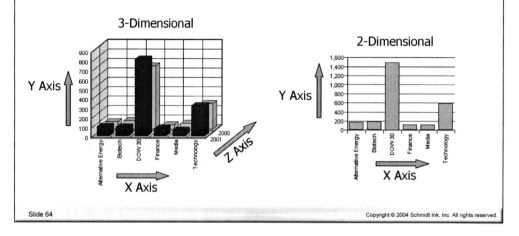

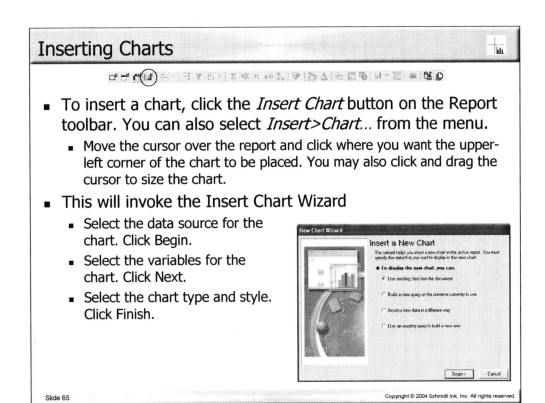

BusinessObjects allows us to insert charts into our reports, but in practice, we usually just convert crosstabs and tables to charts and then modify the chart with the Format Chart dialog.

1. Open Ex 02 04.rep.
2. Click on the Insert a Chart report tab to activate it.
3. Select *Insert>Chart...* from the menu.
4. Move the cursor over the report and it will change into the insert chart cursor.
5. Click where the upper-left corner of the chart will be placed and drag a rectangle before releasing the mouse button. This allows you to determine the size of the chart.
6. Select Use existing data from the Insert Chart Wizard.
7. Select Portfolio Name and Revenue/Expense.
8. Click Next>.
9. Select Pie in the chart types.
10. Select one of the Pie Chart Styles.
11. Click Finish.

- Using the wizard can be a little awkward, especially when we may have a table on our report that contains all of the columns that we want to chart.

  - To convert a table or crosstab to a chart, right-click on the structure and select Turn to Chart from the pop-up menu. You can also select *Format>Turn to Chart* from the application menu.

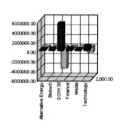

  - To format the labels, click on a label and select Format>Axis Label from the menu. The chart can also be resized, so that more of the axis values will be displayed.

Converting tables to charts is very convenient, because the table may already contain all of the values that we want to include in the chart.

3-D Pie Chart

1. Click on the Convert to Chart report tab to activate it.

2. Click on the top table to select it.

3. Right-click on the table and select *Turn to Chart…*

4. The 3-D Pie type may already be selected, since this is the default for converting a two dimension table. If this type is not selected, select it.

5. Select one of the 3-D Pie Chart styles.

6. Click OK.

3-D Column Chart

1. Right-click on the crosstab report structure.

2. Select Turn to Chart from the pop-up menu.

3. The 3-D Column type may be selected, since this is the default for crosstabs. If it is not selected, select 3-D Column.

4. Select one of the 3-D chart styles.

5. Click OK.

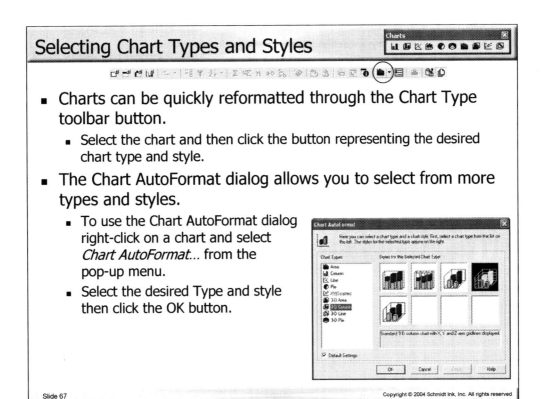

Both of the above methods allow you to quickly change a chart's type and style. The chart toolbar button is a subset of the AutoFormat dialog, which means that the Chart AutoFormat dialog has the same options, plus a few more.

Chart Type Toolbar Button

1. Click on the pie chart.
2. Click the down arrow to the right of the Chart Type toolbar button.
3. Apply a new type and style to the chart.
4. Repeat for various other types.

AutoFormat Dialog

1. Right-click on the 3-D column chart and select Chart AutoFormat…
2. Click the 2-D Column type. ▮▮ Column
3. Click the side-by-side style.
4. Click OK.

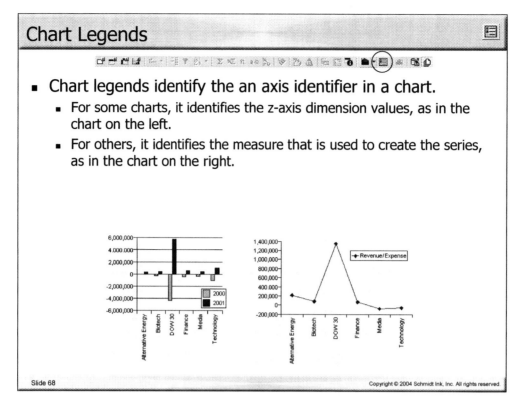

It is often necessary to insert a legend into a chart. Legends can either identify the dimension values or the measure series.

1. Click on either chart.
2. Select *Insert>Chart Components>Legend* from the menu.

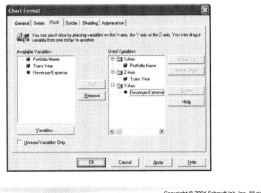
Earlier, we learned how to switch the rows and columns in a crosstab. We use the same methods (Pivot tab - Slice and Dice) to swap the axis dimensions in a chart.

Pivot Tab Method

1. Click on the Switch Axes report tab to activate it.

2. Right-click on the chart and select *Format>Chart...* from the menu.

3. Click the Pivot tab to activate it.

4. In the Used Variables section, drag the Trans Year object to the X-Axis folder.

5. Drag the Portfolio Name object to the Z-Axis folder.

6. Click OK.

Slice and Dice Method

1. Select *Analysis>Slice and Dice...* from the menu.

2. In the Block Structure section, drag the Portfolio Name object, hold down the [Shift] key, and drop the object directly on the Trans Year object. (The objects should trade places)

3. Click Apply.

4. Click the **x** in the upper-right corner to dismiss the panel.

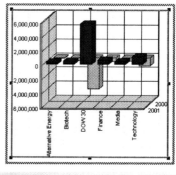
The two containers often confuse people when they start working with charts. It is important to realize that the outer container contains the chart, legend, and title, while the inner-chart container only holds the chart control.

1. Click on the Chart Container report tab to activate it.

2. Click in the middle of the chart. You will see that the chart itself is framed and the outer container is also framed.

3. Click and drag one of the black nodes, on the inner selection, to further inside the chart. (You should notice that the outer container did not resize)

4. Click and drag one of the black nodes, on the inner selection, to outside the outer chart container. (You should notice that the outer container will now resize to accommodate for the larger chart)

5. Click on the outer frame. Click on one of the black nodes and drag it to enlarge the container. (You should notice that the inner chart did not resize)

6. Right-click on the chart. Select Format>Chart. Click on the General tab to activate it. Select Adjust plot area to chart size. Click OK. (You should notice the inner chart sized to the outer frame)

7. Click on the outer frame. Drag one of the black nodes to make the chart smaller. (You should notice that the inside container resized to accommodate to outer frame)

- We often want to plot more than one measure on a chart.
    - For example, Revenue/Expense and Number of Transactions.
    - To add another measure to a chart
        - Right-click on the chart and select *Format Chart...* from the menu
        - Right-click on Group 1 and select Variables…
        - Select the variable to add from the Variables dialog

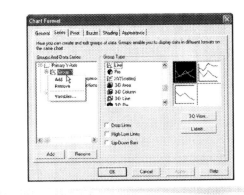 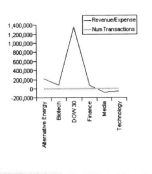

Multiple measure charts allow us to compare two different series. For example, we may want to look at revenue and number of shares. In more advanced reports, we can look at profit and risk. In any case, multiple measure charts can help us to better understand our business.

- We also may prefer to chart the two different measures using different chart types and styles
  - For example, Revenue/Expense as a line and Num Transactions as a column. To have different chart types, a new group must be added.
  - To add another group to a chart
    - Click the Add button to add Group 2 to the chart
    - Select a chart type and style for the new group
    - Drag the Num Transactions object to the new group

 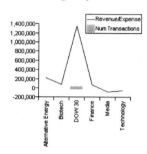

72

- Many times the magnitude of the measures may significantly differ. Therefore, the need for a secondary Y-Axis.
  - For example, the revenue/expense values are so much larger than the number of transactions that the transactions do not even show on the chart
  - To utilize the secondary Y-Axis
    - Simply drag a group from the primary Y-Axis to the Secondary Y-Axis

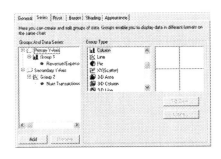 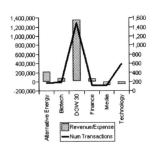

1. Click on the Multiple Measure Chart report tab.
2. Right-click on the chart and select Format>Chart from the menu.
3. Click on the Series tab to activate it.
4. Click on the plus sign (+) in front of Group 1 in the primary Y-Axis.
5. Right-click on the Group 1 folder and select Variables…
6. Select Abs Num Shares and click OK.
7. Click OK in the Chart Format dialog. (If you look at the chart, you may not even notice the number of shares. The reason for this is that the revenue magnitude is so much larger. Therefore, we need to use a different axis to measure the number of shares)
8. Right-click on the chart and select Format>Chart…
9. Click on the Series tab. Click on the Secondary Y-Axis folder and click the Add button. This will add Group 2 to that folder.
10. Open Group 1 and drag the Abs Num Shares object to Group 2.
11. Click on Group 2 and change it's type to Line.
12. Click OK.

Applying Templates

- Since many of our reports contain the same basic objects and/or formats, BusinessObjects allows us to apply existing templates to our reports.
  - To select a template for a new report, select the Select a Template option in the New Report Wizard.
  - To apply a template to an existing report, select *Format>Report>Apply Template...* from the menu.

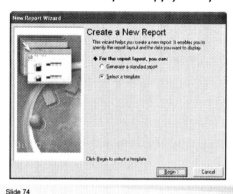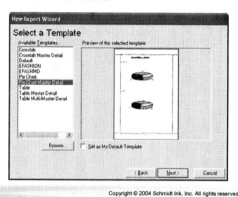

Many companies use templates to create a default look for their reports. Many departments within companies use these formats to identify their reports, thus allowing the departments to build credibility within the company.

Company formats usually include a corporate logo, a department logo, the last execution date, formatted page numbers, and even a field that displays if the document is fully refreshed.

1. Open Ex 02 05.rep.
2. Select Format>Reports>Apply Template... from the menu.
3. Select a template and apply it to the report.
4. Repeat steps 2 & 3.

Saving Templates

- You can create templates by simply saving your document as a template.
  - Reports with multiple tables, usually do not make good templates, because BusinessObjects may populate the structures improperly.
- To save a document as a template
  - Select File>Save As... from the menu
  - Select the Templates directory in the Save As dialog
  - Select BusinessObjects Templates (*.ret) as the File as Type field.

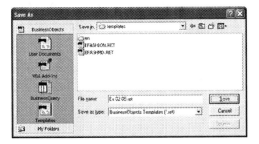

75

First Level Course for BusinessObjects Reporter

Sorts, Filters, Ranks, Alerts and Groups

Introduction

- Now that we can create report structures, we can enhance our reports by sorting, filtering, and ranking the results. We can also apply alerters that allow us to emphasize information based on the values in a report.
- In this chapter we will learn how
  - To place, remove, modify, and locate sorts in a report.
  - To filter data so that only the information of interest is visible.
  - To filter or rank values on there relative strengths in a document.
  - To place alerters that emphasize the information in a report.

Sorts

- Sorts allow us to arrange information in descending or ascending order. We can even, create custom sorts.
- We can sort the
    - Rows of a table by any combination of columns.
    - Rows and/or columns of a crosstab. We can also sort the body.
    - Chart axis values and the magnitude of the graphic elements.

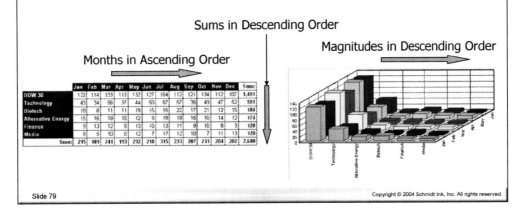

We can sort almost any aspect of a report. BusinessObjects is very flexible in this way, although it may not always be obvious how to accomplish the sort. In this chapter, we will talk about the various ways to apply a sort.

- The simplest way to apply a sort is to click on the value to be sorted and then click on one of the sort toolbar buttons.
  - The disadvantage of this method is that it is difficult to determine which of the other structure elements already have a sort applied to them.
  - The sort toolbar buttons will not override existing sorts, and preexisting sorts have priority over newly applied sorts.
  - If an object already has a sort applied to it, the sort toolbar button will be depressed.
  - The default sort is applied to the first column, then to the second, ...

	Jan	Feb	Mar	Apr	May	Jun	Sum:
Alternative Energy	15.00	15.00	19.00	15.00	12.00	9.00	85.00
Biotech	18.00	8.00	11.00	11.00	19.00	15.00	82.00
DOW 30	122.00	114.00	133.00	113.00	132.00	127.00	741.00
Finance	9.00	13.00	12.00	9.00	13.00	10.00	66.00
Media	8.00	5.00	10.00	8.00	12.00	7.00	50.00
Technology	43.00	34.00	56.00	37.00	44.00	50.00	264.00
Sum:	215.00	189.00	241.00	193.00	232.00	218.00	1,288.00

	Jan	Feb	Mar	Apr	May	Jun	Sum:
DOW 30	122.00	114.00	133.00	113.00	132.00	127.00	741.00
Technology	43.00	34.00	56.00	37.00	44.00	50.00	264.00
Alternative Energy	15.00	15.00	19.00	15.00	12.00	9.00	85.00
Biotech	18.00	8.00	11.00	11.00	19.00	15.00	82.00
Finance	9.00	13.00	12.00	9.00	13.00	10.00	66.00
Media	8.00	5.00	10.00	8.00	12.00	7.00	50.00
Sum:	215.00	189.00	241.00	193.00	232.00	218.00	1,288.00

Slide 80

The Sort toolbar buttons allows us a quick way to sort an object. However, they do not override existing sorts on other objects in the same report. Therefore, the buttons will only allow sorts within existing sorts in the report.

1. Open Ex 03 01.rep.
2. Click on the Report to Sort report tab to activate it.
3. Click on any value in the Portfolio Name column.
4. Click the small down arrow to the right of the Insert Sort toolbar button.
5. Click on the Apply Descending Sort button.
6. Click any value in the Trans Year column.
7. Click the Apply Descending Sort toolbar button. (This will cause the years to sort within the portfolio names, but not effect the portfolio name sort)
8. Click on any value in Portfolio Name column.
   (Notice that the Insert Sort toolbar button is depressed)
9. Click on the depressed Insert Descending Sort button. (This will turn off the sort. Notice that the table is not sorted by Trans Year first, then by Portfolio Name)

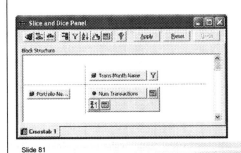 Another method of sorting is to use the Slice and Dice Panel.

- To use the panel, select the structure to sort and then select *Analysis>Slice and Dice...* from the menu.
- Select the element to sort in the panel and then click the Sort toolbar button. To change the orientation, double-click the sort icon on the sorted element.
- The disadvantage of this method is that it does not display sorts that have been place on totals or hidden sorts, which are sorts placed on hidden elements of a structure.

	Jan	Feb	Mar	Apr	May	Jun	Sum:
DOW 30	122.00	114.00	133.00	113.00	132.00	127.00	741.00
Technology	43.00	34.00	56.00	37.00	44.00	50.00	264.00
Alternative Energy	15.00	15.00	19.00	15.00	12.00	9.00	85.00
Biotech	18.00	8.00	11.00	11.00	19.00	15.00	82.00
Finance	9.00	13.00	12.00	9.00	13.00	10.00	66.00
Media	8.00	5.00	10.00	8.00	12.00	7.00	50.00
Sum:	215.00	189.00	241.00	193.00	232.00	218.00	1.288.00

The Slice and Dice Panel allows us to view and remove most existing sorts, and to apply new ones.

1. Click on the report to select it.
2. Click the Slice and Dice toolbar button.
3. Click on the sort icon that is placed on the Trans Year object and drag it to the Available Variables section to remove it from the Block Structure.
4. Click on the Portfolio Name object to select it.
5. Click the Apply Sort toolbar button in the panel. (This will place the sort icon on the Portfolio Name object)
6. Double-click the sort icon on the Portfolio Name object. (This will change its orientation from ascending to Descending)
7. Click Apply to apply the changes.
8. Dismiss the panel by clicking the **x** in the upper-right corner of the dialog.

- The previous two methods did apply sorts to elements within a structure. However, both methods do not display all of the sorts that may apply to a structure.
    - The Sorts dialog will display all effective sorts in the Current Sorts portion of the dialog.
    - It will also display if a sort is a custom sort in the Sort Definition portion.
    - It is very important to examine this dialog when a report structure is not behaving properly. Examples of bad behavior could be
        - Not sorting as expected.
        - Not breaking as expected.
- To open this dialog, select *Format>Sorts...*

The two previous methods work for most sorts. However, when there is a need to analyze all sorts placed on a report structure, there is no better way to examine all of the sorts than the Sorts dialog. This dialog will list and prioritize all sorts that effect a selected structure.

1. Click anywhere on the table to select it.
2. Select *Format>Sorts...* from the menu.
3. The Current Sorts window lists the current sort on Portfolio Name.
4. Click the Add... button.
5. Select Trans Year and click OK.
6. Make sure that the Trans Year object is selected in the Current Sorts window, and click the Descending button. (Notice the arrow preceding the object is now pointing down)
7. Click the Move Up button to make Trans Year the first sort in the list. (The report will now sort Trans Year descending, then sort Portfolio Name descending. The rest of the columns will sort in the order in which they appear in the table)

Custom Sorts

- Custom sorts allow us to determine the sort order for the values of an object.
    - To define a custom sort, click on the object.
    - Click the Custom Sort toolbar button.
    - Drag the values to the desired sort order. You can also use one of the predefined sorts in the Sort Option drop down list.
    - You can also apply custom sorts in the Sorts dialog.
- Custom sorts will apply to all instances of the object in the report.

Many times there is a need to define the sort order for the values of an object. Companies may like to see the departments listed in a certain order, they may want their products listed from most significant to least, or the names of months sorted not in alphabetical order, but in chronological order.

1. Click on the Custom Sort report tab to activate it.

2. Click on any of the month names along the X-axis of the chart.

3. Select *Format>Sorts...* from the menu.

4. Click the *Add...* button and select Trans Month Name, then click OK.

5. Select the Custom option in the Sort Definition section.

6. Click the Values... button.

7. Click the Jan value and click Move Up until it is the first value.

8. Click and drag the Feb value to right on top of the Jan value. (Values dropped on other values will be placed below the value in the list.)

9. Click on the drop list in the Sort Option section and select Month. (This will arrange the entire list in chronological order)

10. Click OK in the Custom Sort dialog.

11. Click OK in the Sorts dialog.

12. Notice the Trans Years are no longer sorted correctly. Go back to the Sort dialog and make Trans Year the first sort.

- Filters allow us to make selected information in a report or report structure visible, while hiding other information in the report. This allows us to
  - Isolate information in large reports.
  - Perform calculations that compare visible information with hidden information.
  - Have a large query that returns a superset of data, then display subsets of the information in different report structures.

- Filters can not be placed on aggregated data.
  - Sum, min, max...

Portfolio Name	Trans Year	Revenue/ Expense
Alternative Energ	2000	-89,221
Alternative Energ	2001	303,886
Biotech	2000	-369,888
Biotech	2001	449,314
DOW 30	2000	-4,385,413
DOW 30	2001	5,736,866
Finance	2000	-507,101
Finance	2001	574,563
Media	2000	-465,394
Media	2001	386,854
Technology	2000	-1,116,767
Technology	2001	1,059,497

Portfolio Name	Trans Year	Revenue/ Expense
Biotech	2000	-369,888
Biotech	2001	449,314
Finance	2000	-507,101
Finance	2001	574,563
Media	2000	-465,394
Media	2001	386,854

Many companies use filters as often as sorts. They use them to hide information that is necessary for calculations in a report, but not necessary to display in a report. They also use them for many other reasons, therefore it is import to become very proficient at creating and placing filters.

- The Insert Filter toolbar button allows us to quickly insert a filter into a report structure.
  - To insert the filter, click on any data cell in a column
  - Click the Insert Filter button
  - Select the values to display
  - Click OK

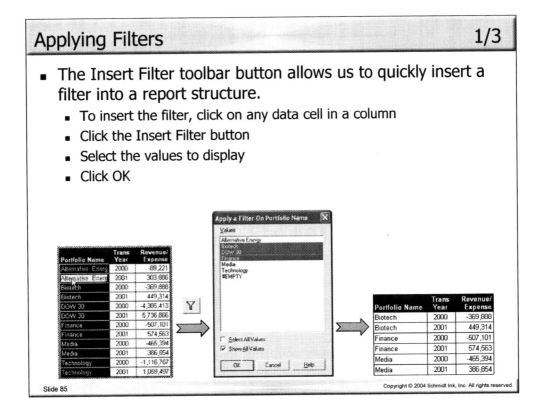

Filters allow us to focus on specific information in a report, while hiding unnecessary data.

1. Open Ex 03 02.rep.
2. Click on the Report to Filter tab to activate the report.
3. Click on any of the Portfolio Master cells.
4. Click the Apply Filter toolbar button.
5. Select all of the Portfolio Names, except Alternative Energy.
6. Click OK,

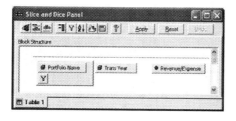

Another way to insert a filter is to use Slice and Dice

- The Insert Filter toolbar button works well, but it does not show you existing filters or allow you to modify a filter.
- The Slice and Dice panel will display existing filters on objects in a report structure. Note the filter icon on the Portfolio Name object.
- To modify the filter, double-click on the filter icon and reselect values.
- To place a new sort, select an object in the panel, and then click the filter toolbar button in the panel. Select the desired values then click OK.

Portfolio Name	Trans Year	Revenue/ Expense
Biotech	2000	-369,888
Biotech	2001	449,314
Finance	2000	-507,101
Finance	2001	574,563
Media	2000	-465,394
Media	2001	386,854

The Slice and Dice panel allows us to see most of the filters that effect the report structures in our documents.

1. Click on the Slice and Dice toolbar button.
2. Notice the filter icon on the Portfolio Name object in the Section window of the panel.
3. Click on the Trans Year object in the Block Structure section. (Notice that it got a little bigger. This means that it is the currently selected item.
4. Click the Apply Filter toolbar button in the panel.
5. Select 2001 from the Apply a Filter dialog.
6. Click OK.
7. Double-click on the filter icon on the Portfolio Name object in the Section window.
8. Hold down the [Ctrl] key and click on Technology to deselect it.
9. Click the OK button.
10. Click Apply.
11. Click the **x** in the upper-right corner of the dialog to dismiss it.

- The Filters dialog displays all sorts on a report structure, and also any Global filters that may be applied.
  - To use the Filters dialog, click on any report structure, and then select Format>Filters... from the menu.
- With this dialog you can add, remove, modify, and even create custom filters.

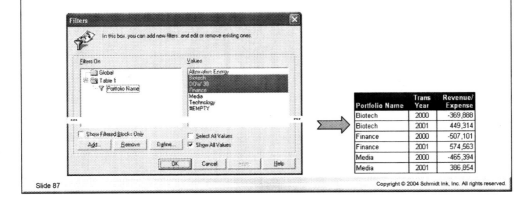

The Filters dialog is more powerful than the Slice and Dice panel, because it shows all filters that affect our report structure - including Global Filters, and filters on deleted and hidden objects.

1. Click on the table to select it.
2. Select *Format>Filters...* from the menu.
3. Expand both filter folders in the Filters On section of the dialog. (We should see the filter that we placed on Portfolio Name in the Global folder, and the filter on Trans Year in the Table 1 folder)
4. Click on the Portfolio Name filter in the Global folder. (Notice that the object values are displayed in the Values section and the currently filtered values are selected)
5. Reselect the Portfolio Names values in any combination.
6. Click OK to dismiss the dialog and to update any filters.

Global Filters

- Notice that there are two folders in the Filters On section of the dialog.
  - The Global section displays any filters that apply to the entire report. This includes any and all report structures.
  - To make a local filter global, simply drag the filter from the local folder (Table 1, in this case) and drag it to the Global folder.
  - The previous two methods of applying filters will not display any global filters that are applied to a report.
- It is always a good idea to check for global filters when a report has unexpected behavior.

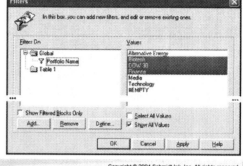

Global filters apply to the entire report. They are very convenient if you want to apply the same filter to all report components.

88

Adding a Filter with the Filters Dialog

- To add a filter to a report structure
  - Click on the report structure.
  - Select *Format>Filters...* from the menu.
  - Select the structure in the Filters On list.
  - Click the Add... button and select a new object to filter.
  - Click Ok.
  - Select the values from the Values list.

The Variable(s) to Filter dialog allows us to place filters on objects that are not part of the report.

1. Open Ex 03 02.rep.
2. Click on the Global Filter report tab to select it.
3. Select *Format>Filters...* from the menu.
4. Select the Global folder in the Filters On section.
5. Click the *Add...* button. (Notice that you can place filters on objects that are not even in the current report)
6. Select Portfolio Name.
7. Click OK to dismiss the Variable(s) to Filter dialog.
8. Select all of the names except DOW 30. (Hold down the [Ctrl] key to select multiple values)
9. Click OK.
10. Select *Insert>Special Field>Global Filters* from the menu.
11. Click on the report where you want the upper-left corner of the cell to be.
12. Size the cell to display all of the filtered values.

Removing a Filter with the Filters Dialog

- To remove a filter from a report
  - Click on the report structure.
  - Select *Format>Filters...* from the menu.
  - Select the filter in the Filters On list.
  - Click the Remove button.
  - Click Ok.

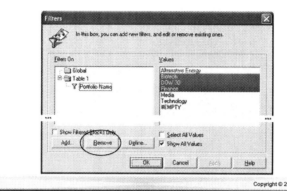

Slide 90

Copyright © 2004 Schmidt Ink, Inc. All rights reserved.

To remove a filter, simply select it and click the Remove button.

1. Select *Format>Filters...* from the menu.
2. Select the Portfolio Name filter in the Filters On section.
3. Click the Remove button to delete the filter.

90

Defining Filters with the Filters Dialog

- **The Filters dialog allows us to use a formula to select values.**
    - To show Portfolio Names where revenue is greater than $100,000
        - Click Add... and select the Portfolio Names object. Click OK.
        - Click the Define... button.
        - Use the Filter Editor to create the following formula
            - = <Revenue/Expense> > 100000.
        - Click OK.

Defining a filter formula allows us to select values via a logical formula. Today's business world is volatile and dynamic. Today's best sellers may not be tomorrow's. Therefore, we often need to create dynamic filters that select values based on criteria defined in a formula.

1. Select *Format>Filters...* from the menu.
2. Click the Add... button to display the Variable(s) to Filter dialog.
3. Select the Portfolio Name object and click OK.
4. Click the Define... button to display the Filter Editor.
5. Double-click Revenue In Portfolio Name.
6. Double-click >= in the operators section.
7. Type 100000 in the Formulas section.
   (= < Revenue In Portfolio Name > >= 100000)
8. Click OK.

Ranks

- Ranks are special filters that allow us to filter dimension values based on the ordinal position of a measure relative to the dimension.
    - For example, we can rank the top three portfolios based on the total revenue in a report, as shown below.
    - We can also rank the bottom performers.
    - We can rank by absolute values or by percentage of total number of values (percentiles).

Portfolio Name	Trans Year	Revenue/ Expense
Alternative Energy	2000	-89,221
Alternative Energy	2001	303,886
Biotech	2000	-369,888
Biotech	2001	449,314
DOW 30	2000	-4,385,413
DOW 30	2001	5,736,866
Finance	2000	-507,101
Finance	2001	574,563
Media	2000	-465,394
Media	2001	386,854
Technology	2000	-1,116,767
Technology	2001	1,059,497

Top three portfolios

Portfolio Name	Trans Year	Revenue/ Expense
DOW 30	2000	-4,385,413
DOW 30	2001	5,736,866
Alternative Energy	2000	-89,221
Alternative Energy	2001	303,886
Biotech	2000	-369,888
Biotech	2001	449,314
	Sum:	1,645,543

Ranks are special filters that filter based on the top or bottom values of a measure that is related to the ranked dimension.

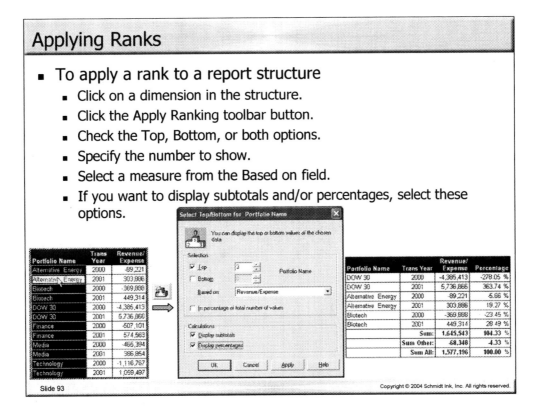

Applying Ranks

- To apply a rank to a report structure
    - Click on a dimension in the structure.
    - Click the Apply Ranking toolbar button.
    - Check the Top, Bottom, or both options.
    - Specify the number to show.
    - Select a measure from the Based on field.
    - If you want to display subtotals and/or percentages, select these options.

1. Open Ex 03 02.rep.
2. Click on the Table to Rank report tab.
3. Click on a Portfolio Industry value in the first table.
4. Click the Apply Ranking toolbar button.
5. Select the Top option and enter a 3 in the field following it.
6. Make sure Revenue/Expense is selected in the Based on field.
7. Select Display Subtotals and Display Percentages.
8. Click OK

Ranks and Breaks

- If you apply a rank to a structure with breaks
  - You can display the subtotals and percentages for each of the ranked dimensions, as shown below.
  - If you apply the break after applying the rank, then the subtotals will not show the rank percentages.
    - If this happens, simply reapply the rank and it will populate the subtotals and percentages for each ranked dimension value.

Portfolio Name	Trans Year	Revenue/Expense	Percentage
DOW 30	2000	-4,385,413	-324.50 %
	2001	5,736,866	424.50 %
DOW 30	Sum:	1,351,453	85.69 %
Alternative Energy	2000	-89,221	-41.56 %
	2001	303,886	141.56 %
Alternative Energy	Sum:	214,665	13.61 %
	Sum:	1,566,118	99.30 %
	Sum Other:	11,078	0.70 %
	Sum All:	1,577,196	100.00 %

1. Click on any Portfolio Company value in the second table.
2. Click the Apply Ranking toolbar button.
3. Select the Top option and enter a 2 in the field following it.
4. Make sure Revenue/Expense is selected in the Based on field.
5. Select Display Subtotals and Display Percentages.
6. Click OK

This exercise applied the ranking to a table with breaks. This caused the top two portfolio companies in each break to be displayed.

Alerters

- Alerters also us to highlight or modify information in a report base on a logical formula.
    - We may highlight rows in a table where the revenue is less than zero, as shown below.
    - We can replace values with text or values from another object.
    - We can format any attribute of a cell based on values in a report.

Portfolio Name	Revenue/ Expense
Alternative Energy	214,665
Biotech	79,426
DOW 30	1,351,453
Finance	67,462
Media	79,540
Technology	57,270

Alerters are used in many ways in different companies. They are flexible and allow people to get creative when applying them.

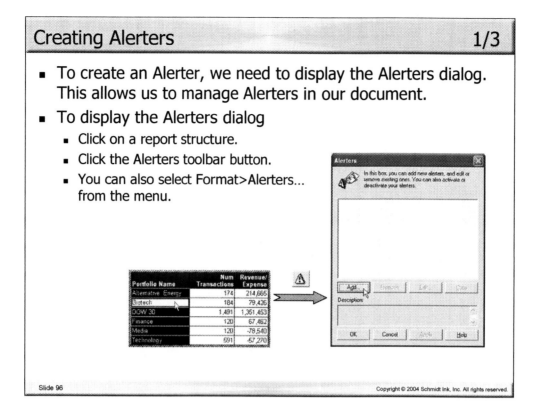

- To create an Alerter, we need to display the Alerters dialog. This allows us to manage Alerters in our document.
- To display the Alerters dialog
    - Click on a report structure.
    - Click the Alerters toolbar button.
    - You can also select Format>Alerters... from the menu.

The Alerters dialog displays all of the alerters in a document. This allows you to edit, delete, or apply existing alerters to report structures in any report in a document.

1. Open Ex 03 02.rep.
2. Click the Creating Alerters report tab to activate it.
3. Click any value in the Portfolio Name column.
4. Click the Alerters toolbar button.

- ■ **The Add... button displays the Edit Alerters dialog.**
  - ■ With this dialog, we create new and modify existing alerters.
- ■ **The definition tab allows us to name and describe an alerter.**
  - ■ The name and description of the alerter help us to determine the purpose of an alerter. In a report with many alerters it is very necessary to fill in these fields to help others to understand the alerters.

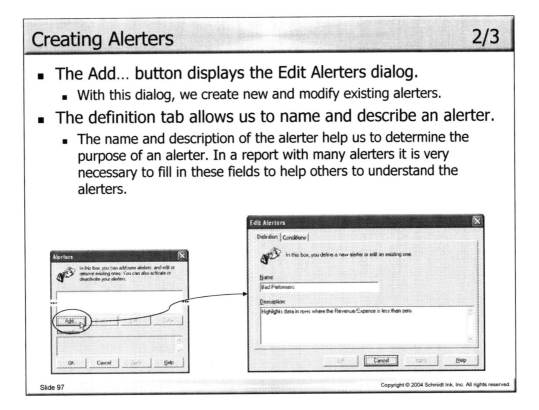

The Definition tab allows us to name and describe our alerters. This is very important, if we want to remember how our alerters function - without having to examine the logic each time we revisit our alerters. It is also good to let others know the purpose of an alerter.

1. Click on the Definition tab to activate it.

2. Name our Alerter – Portfolios with over 200,000 in Revenue.

3. Describe our Alerter – Highlights cells where the portfolio has done more than 200,000 in revenue.

- The Condition tab allows us to define the logic and the result of the alerter.
  - Select a variable from the Variable to Compare field dropdown list.
  - Select a logical operator from the Operator 1 field.
  - Select a value from the Value 1 drop list or just type in a value.
  - Click the down arrow on the result field to select the result type.

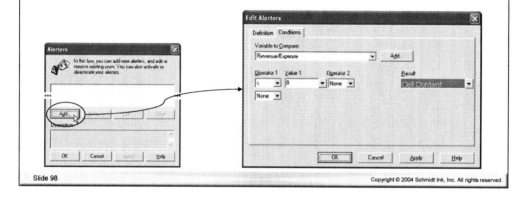

The Condition tab allows us to define the behavior of our alerter.

1. Click on the Condition tab to activate it.
2. Make sure Revenue/Expense is in the Variable to Compare field.
3. Select >= in the Operator 1 drop-down list.
4. Type 200000 in the Value 1 field.
5. Leave None in the Operator 2 field.
6. Click the down arrow to the right of the Result field and select Format...
7. Click the Shading tab to activate it.
8. Click on the white rectangle in the Foreground color section.
9. Click the light blue color in the Color dialog and click OK.
10. Select Solid in the Shading list.
11. Click the Font tab to activate it.
12. Select Automatic in the color section.
13. Click OK.
14. Click OK in the Edit Alerters dialog.

Alerters with Multiple States

- Alerters can have up to five states and each state can be defined by an absolute (Year = 2000) or a range (Revenue > 0 and Revenue < 1,000,000).
  - To define multiple states, select an operator in the Operator 1 field and another row will be added to the dialog. We can have up to five states.
  - To define a range, select an operator in the Operator 2 field.

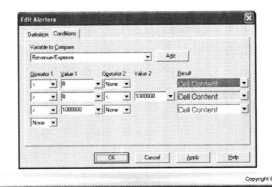

1. Click any Portfolio Name value in the table.
2. Click the Alerters toolbar button.
3. Select our alerter in the alerter list.
4. Click the Edit… button.
5. Select >= in the second row Operator 1 drop list.
6. Type 0 in the second row Operator 1 field.
7. Select < in the second row Operator 2 field.
8. Type 200000 in the second row Value 2 field.
9. Click the down arrow to the right of the second row Results field.
10. Select Format… from the menu.
11. Click on the Shading tab to activate it.
12. Click on the white rectangle in the Foreground Color section.
13. Select light green from the Color dialog and click OK.
14. Click on the Font tab to activate it.
15. Select the Automatic option in the Color section.
16. Click OK.
17. Click OK in the Alerter dialog.
18. Click OK in the Alerters dialog.

Alerters Values

- In the previous two examples, we typed values into the Value 1 field. However, there are two other options
  - List of Values
    This allows us to select from the values of the variable. This option works best with Dates and Text dimension values.
  - Variables…
    We can compare the variable to compare to other variables in the report.

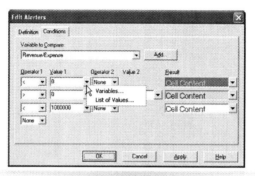

100

Alerter Results

- Alerters can format a cell, replace cell contents with text, and/or replace cell contents with another variable.
  - To select a result, click the down arrow to the right of the result and select
    - Format to display the Cell Format dialog.
    - Text to display a dialog that will allow you to enter the substitute text.
    - Variables for a list of substitute variables.

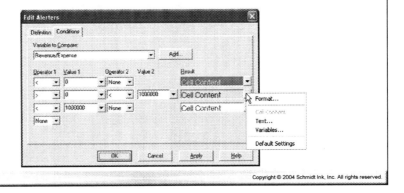

101

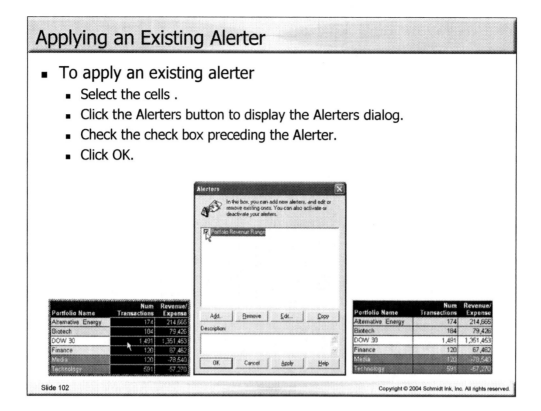

Applying an Existing Alerter

- To apply an existing alerter
  - Select the cells .
  - Click the Alerters button to display the Alerters dialog.
  - Check the check box preceding the Alerter.
  - Click OK.

Sometimes an alerter looks good when it is applied to a signal column and sometimes it looks best when it is applied to the entire row.

1. Select an entire row in our table.
2. Click the Alerters button. (Notice that the box preceding our alerter in the list is grayed out. This means that it is applied to some cells in the selection, but not all)
3. Click the little box preceding our alerter, until there is a little check in the box.
4. Click OK to apply the alerter to the selection.
5. Click off the report so that you can see the results.

Alerter Legend

- If an alerter applies to values of a dimension, it is sometimes good to place a legend that defines what the different alerter formats mean.
- To create a legend
  - Make a table that displays the dimension values.
  - Apply the alerter to the values.
- In the example below, I just copied the table and deleted the two other columns, thus leaving only the year column.

Portfolio Name	Trans Year	Revenue/Expense	Legend
Alternative Energy	2000	-89,221.30	2000
Alternative Energy	2001	303,895.90	2001
Biotech	2000	369,888.40	
Biotech	2001	449,314.10	
DOW 30	2000	-4,385,412.50	
DOW 30	2001	5,736,865.50	
Finance	2000	-507,100.70	
Finance	2001	574,563.00	
Media	2000	-485,393.90	
Media	2001	386,853.60	
Technology	2000	-1,116,787.25	
Technology	2001	1,059,497.45	

Sometimes a legend is necessary to inform viewers of a report what the alerter formats divulge. The easiest method is for alerters placed on dimension values. In these cases, we just copy the table and delete all columns, except the column with the alerter value.

1. Open Ex 03 02.rep.
2. Click on the Alerter Legend tab to activate it.
3. Copy the table and paste it to the right.
4. Delete the Portfolio Name, Num Transactions, and Revenue/Expense columns.

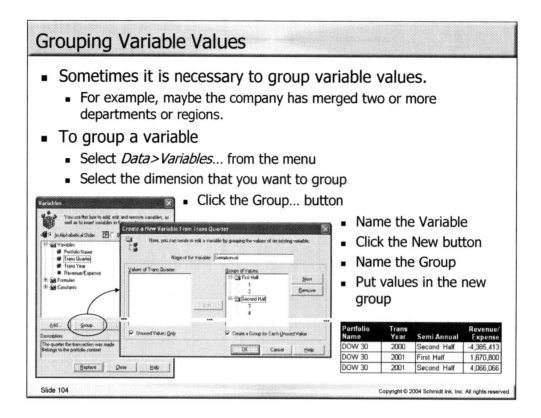

Grouping Variable Values

- Sometimes it is necessary to group variable values.
    - For example, maybe the company has merged two or more departments or regions.
- To group a variable
    - Select *Data>Variables...* from the menu
    - Select the dimension that you want to group
        - Click the Group... button
- Name the Variable
- Click the New button
- Name the Group
- Put values in the new group

Grouping values allows us create new variables by grouping the values of an existing object.

1. Open Ex 03 02.rep.
2. Click the Grouping tab to select it.
3. Click on any value in the Trans Quarter column.
4. Select *Data>Variables...* from the menu.
5. If the Trans Quarter object is not selected, click on it.
6. Click the Group... button.
7. Name the variable: Semi Annual.
8. Click the New button and name the new folder: 1st Half.
9. Double-click the 1 and the 2 in the Values of Trans Quarter section. (This will place both values in our new folder)
10. Click the new button and name the new folder: 2nd Half.
11. Double-click the 3 and the 4 in the Values of Trans Quarter section.
12. Click OK to create the new variable.
13. Click Replace to replace the Trans Quarter column with Semi Annual.

Grouping vs. If-Then-Else

- In the previous slide, we used the grouping function to group the quarter values into semi-annual groups. Another way to perform the same functionality is with the following formula:
  - = If <Trans Quarter> InList (1 ,2) Then "First Half"
    Else If <Trans Quarter> InList (3 , 4) Then "Second Half"
    Else FormatNumber(<Trans Quarter> , "0")
  - This is an advanced function that performs the same as grouping
    - Advantage
      It is easily copied to other documents
    - Disadvantage
      It is not graphical
      It is complex

You haven't learned this formula yet, but it is good to talk about it now so that when you do, you will understand.

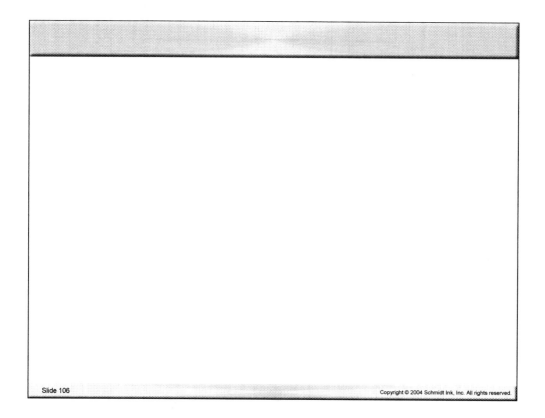

106

First Level Course for BusinessObjects Reporter

Master-Details
And
Breaks

Introduction

- The report structures allow us to see information in our reports. However, information is sometimes more useful if it is organized into groups within our reports
    - For example
        - A report that groups by each portfolio in our universe
        - One that groups by quarters
- Once a information has been organized into groups, we can then analyze the information with aggregates, such as sum, max, min, average, and so forth
- In BusinessObjects, we can organize our information into groups using Master-Details and Breaks

Almost every report has some sort of break in it – either a master detail or a break report. Breaks in data allow us to calculate and display subtotals and other sub-calculations. They also allow us to neatly format groups of dimension values.

Master Detail Reports

- Master detail reports allow us to divide a report into sections
  - Each section is controlled by a dimension value that acts like a filter to show only information that is related to that particular value of the dimension.
  - By default, the master cell value is displayed in a freestanding cell in the section.
  - We can place any report structure in the sections.
    - To the right, we have placed a table and a chart.

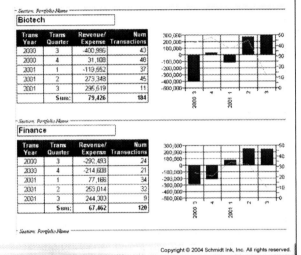

1. Open EX 04 01.rep.
2. Click on the Master Detail report tab to activate it.
3. Browse around the report.
   - Click on a report structure and observe the section delimiters.
   - Notice that there is a chart and a table for each section.

- Master details are created by first selecting a dimension in a report structure and then by clicking the Set as Master toolbar button.
    - We use dimensions, because dimensions are supposed to uniquely identify information, such as Employee ID, Portfolio Name, Dates, and so forth.

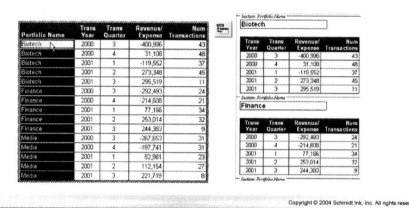

1. Open EX 04 01.rep.

2. Click on the Create Master Detail report tab to activate that report.

3. Click on any value in the Portfolio Name column.

4. Click on it again and drag the value to outside of the report and drop it. (This will create a master detail using Portfolio Name as the section master)

- The Slice and Dice panel allows you to quickly create and modify masters.
  - Place a dimension object in the Section window and click apply to create a master.
  - Place and order multiple dimensions in the Section window to create multiple master reports.

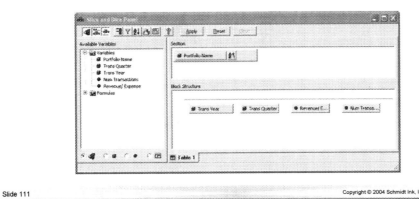

1. Open EX 04 01.rep.
2. Click on the Using Slice and Dice report tab to activate that report.
3. Click on the Slice and Dice toolbar button.
4. Drag Portfolio Name from the Structure window to the Section window.
5. Click Apply.
6. Click the **x** in the upper-right of the dialog to dismiss it.

7. Click on the Slice and Dice toolbar button.
8. Drag the Trans Year object from the Structure window into the Section and drop it.
9. Click Apply.
10. Click the **x** in the upper-right of the dialog to dismiss it.

The second part of this exercise created a multiple master report.

- To sort or filter the sections in a master detail report, we select the master cell, and then use any of the methods we learned in the previous chapter.
  - Filters placed on the master cell become global filters.

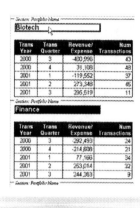

When we sort or filter the sections in a master detail, most of the time, we place the sort or filter on the master cell. Filters on the Master cell become global filters.

Placing a Sort

1. Open EX 04 01.rep.
2. Click on the Sort Masters report tab to activate it.
3. Click on any Portfolio Master cell.
4. Click the Sort Descending (Z-A) toolbar button.

Placing a Filter

1. Click on any Portfolio Name master cell.
2. Select the Insert Filter toolbar button.
3. Select a couple of the values and click OK.

Sorting Master Detail Sections Based on a Measure

- Suppose that you wanted to sort the sections based on the revenue of a section. To do this, we temporarily drag a measure into the section and then sort it.

  - If the sections appear not to sort, then they are probably already sorted by the dimension values, as seen in the Sorts dialog below. If this is the case, simply removed the sort on the dimension.

  - After applying the sort, you may hide the cell with the Format Cell dialog.

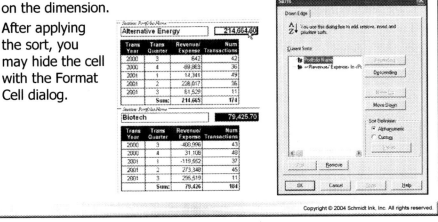

Sometimes we may want to sort the sections based on the value of some other freestanding cell in the section. We can do this by placing the sort on the other cell.

1. Click on any of the Portfolio Name master cells.

2. Select *Format>Sorts...* from the menu.

3. Click on the Portfolio Name sort in the dialog and click Remove.

4. Answer 'Yes' to Do you really want to remove the Sort?

5. Click the Add.. button.

6. Select the Revenue/Expense object. (Notice that it says <Revenue/Expense> In <Portfolio Name>. This means that it will sort using the total revenue for each Portfolio Name)

7. Click the OK button in the Variable(s) to Sort dialog.

8. Click the OK button in the Sorts dialog.

113

Hiding Master Detail Sections

- After creating a master detail report, we may notice that several of the sections contain no data. If this is the case, we may want to hide the section.
  - In the table below, there are no calls for Alternative Energy. To hide this section and others that also have no calls.
  - Click anywhere in the section to select it
  - Select Format>Section...
  - On the General tab, select the Hide Section option
  - Enter this formula = IsNull (<Num Calls>)
  - Click OK

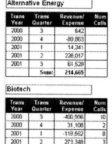

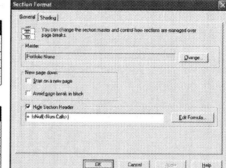

1. Click on the Hide Sections report tab.
2. Click on any report structure in a section.
3. Select *Format>Section...* from the menu.
4. Click on the General tab to activate it.
5. Select the Hide Section option.
6. Click the Edit Formula... button.
7. Open the Logical Functions folder and double-click the IsNull function.
8. Double-click the Num Calls object in the Variables section.
9. Click OK.

10. Click the Map tab in the Report Manager. (Notice that the hidden sections still show in the Hide Sections report. This can be misleading to some viewers of the report. Therefore, it may be better to place a filter on the sections to remove the sections with no calls)
11. Click on a master cell and select *Format>Filters...* from the menu. Click the Add button and select Portfolio Name. Click OK to dismiss the Variables to Filter dialog. Click the Define button. Double-click the Equals operator (=), then the Not operator. Open the Logical Functions folder and double-click IsNull. Double-Click the Num Calls object. Click Ok. Click OK. (You should now notice that the sections with no calls are removed from the Report Manager)

114

Sections and Navigation

- One of the large advantages of a master detail report is that the Report Manager will allow us to easily locate and go to sections within a report.
    - To use the Report Manager to navigate
        - Activate the Map tab.
        - Select the Navigation option located at the bottom of the manager.
- The disadvantage of hiding sections is that they will still be displayed in the Report Manager.
    - They will show formatted as italicized, as seen in the Report Manager in this slide.
    - Perhaps, in these cases it is better to set a filter.

Hidden sections will appear in the Report Manager navigation and also as options in a BusinessObjects report viewed in the WEBI environment. These visible-hidden sections can be confusing to viewers of the report, because they will wonder why the section has been hidden and some may even try to navigate there.

Filtering Empty Sections

- In the previous slide, we hid sections based on if the number of calls were null. Here, we use the Filters dialog to add a filter on the master dimension.
    - Select the Portfolio Name dimension as the object to filter on.
    - Click the *Define...* button to display the Formula Editor.
    - Create the following formula
        - = Not IsNull (<Num Calls>)

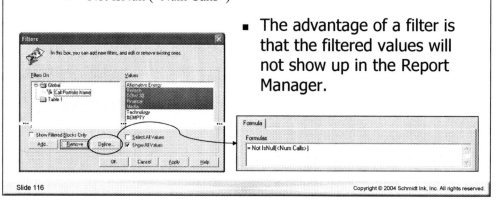

- The advantage of a filter is that the filtered values will not show up in the Report Manager.

We did this in an earlier exercise.

116

Sections and Page Breaks

- You can define how a section will behave when it encounters a page break.
  - Every section can *Start on a new page*.
    - This allows sections in a long report to be easily located.
    - It also makes it easier to separate and distribute sections.
  - If a section is starts on a page that is already populated by at least one section and it is larger than the area left on the page, then it will start on a new page. This is the *Avoid page break in block* option.

    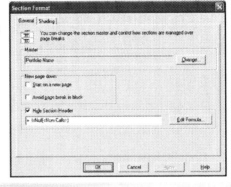

    - This option helps us to avoid having a section at the bottom of a page that is populated with only the table header of a report.

Even the best reports can be ruined, if a page break appears in the middle of a section. With BusinessObjects, we can either start each new section on a new page or, if the break appears in the middle of a section, start that section on a new page.

1. Click on the Page Break report tab to activate it.
2. Select *View>Page Layout* from the menu.
3. Click on any structure in a section.
4. Select *Format>Section…* from the menu.
5. Select the Avoid Page Break in Block option.
6. Click OK. (Scroll to the next page and see that the section does start on a new page)

Section Headers and Footers

- Sections have headers and footers. In the case of a single dimension master detail report, the section header and footer are in the context of the entire report.
- You can hide the header and footer of a section, by double-clicking in the header or footer area and selecting the Hide options at the bottom of the Section Format dialog.

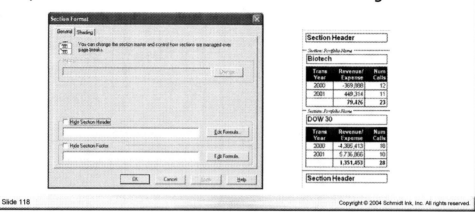

In the case of a single master report, the section footer and header immediately follow and precede the sections on the report.

1. Press the [Ctrl] [Home] key combination to return to the top of the report.

2. Move the cursor over the edge of a table in the report. When the cursor changes into the four-way directional cursor, click and hold the mouse button down.

3. Drag the table to the top of the report, just above the Portfolio Name section. Hold down the [Ctrl] key and release the table. (This will copy the table from inside a section to the section header. The table will now show the totals for the entire report.)

118

Multiple Dimension Master Detail Reports

- Masters can be set on multiple dimensions in a report
  - To set additional masters, simply select the additional dimension, and then click the Set as Master button.
- The report below, has a master set on Portfolio Name and then on Trans Year.
  - Notice that the Portfolio Name section has created a header and a footer where Portfolio Name level summaries can be inserted.
    - These headers or footer can be hidden with the Format Section dialog.

In a multiple master report, the inner section's header is the section above it and the footer is just above the section below it.

1. Open EX 04 01.rep.
2. Click on the Multiple Sections report tab.
3. Drag the smaller table from the report header to just below the year 2001 section. (You will see the delimiters below the table. There is a solid line followed by a line with the Portfolio Name label. Drop it between these lines)

119

Standard Section Format

- The Standard Report Styles dialog allows you to preformat the sections in all of your new master detail documents.
    - Select *Tools>Standard Report Styles...*
    - Since sections contain master cells and sections, the formats differ when different elements are selected. For the section, there is a General tab that allows you to set the New Page Down options.

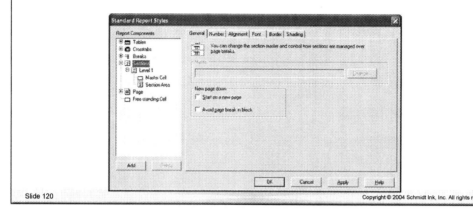

Sections allow for many different report formats, and there are many acceptable variations. For example, some companies like the border around the master cell and some do not. Some like shading in the sections, and most do not. I have seen reports that are made for online viewing, such as in WEBI, and shaded sections are not only attractive, but they can also be functional.

Report Breaks

- Report breaks group information within a table or a crosstab. They do not create report-wide sections, as master details do.
- Since they do not create report sections, we can
  - Have grand totals that are part of the table, as in the table below.
  - Have one table header, where the master detail had one in each section.
  - Have more formatting options.
  - Fold the details of the break and just display the summary footers and header.

Portfolio Name	Trans Year	Trans Quarter	Revenue/ Expense
Biotech	2000	3	-400,996
	2000	4	31,108
	2001	1	-119,552
	2001	2	273,348
	2001	3	295,519
Biotech		Sum:	79,426
DOW 30	2000	3	-2,978,025
	2000	4	-1,807,388
	2001	1	330,350
	2001	2	1,340,450
	2001	3	4,086,066
DOW 30		Sum:	1,351,453
		Sum:	1,430,879

Inserting Report Breaks

- To insert a break
  - Select a dimension in a table or crosstab.
  - Click the Insert Break button.
- Notice that the break created break footers identified by the value of the dimension. In this footer we can insert summary information, such as sums, averages, minimums, maximums and so forth.

Inserting a break is as easy as selecting a dimension value and clicking the Insert Break button

1. Open Ex 04 02.rep.
2. Click on the Break report tab to activate it.
3. Click on any value in the Portfolio Name column.
4. Select *Insert>Break* from the menu.

Break Footer and Header Calculations

- When a break is applied to a table, the aggregate functions will automatically populate the footers of the breaks.
- To apply an aggregate function
  - Click on one of the three aggregate function buttons
  - Or, select Data>Calculations>*Aggregate Function* from the menu.
    - Where aggregate function is Sum, Count, Min, Max, Average, etc.

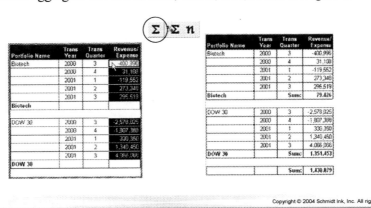

Breaks do not automatically insert calculations into a table, but they do place footers that can be populated with calculations.

1. Click on any value in the Revenue/Expense column.

2. Click the Insert Sum toolbar button.

3. Make sure a Revenue/Expense value is selected and select *Data>Calculations>Percentage* from the menu. (This will place percentages in the footers of the report)

Formatting Breaks

- We have many formatting options for breaks. To format a break, we use the Breaks dialog.
    - To display the Breaks dialog, click on a table and select *Format>Breaks...* from the menu.
    - If there is more than one break in the table, select a break to format from the list.
- With the breaks dialog, we can
    - Show and hide headers and footers.
    - Remove duplicate break values.
    - Center break values.
    - Fold the rows in a break.
    - Define value-based breaks.
    - Define the break behavior when the column encounters a page break.

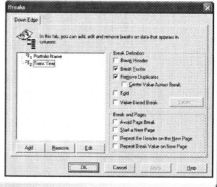

1. Open Ex 04 02.rep.

2. Click on the Format Breaks report tab to activate it.

3. Click anywhere on the table to select it.

4. Select *Format>Breaks...* from the menu.

5. Select the Center Value Across Break option.

6. Click OK. (This will center the break across the rows in the break. This is probably not a good option for breaks with many rows)

7. Click anywhere on the table to select it.

8. Select Format>Table... from the menu.

9. Select the Show Header option and click OK. (Notice that the table header row is not formatted the same as the break headers)

10. Select the entire break header row. (You can hold down the [Ctrl] key and select on each cell or use some other method)

11. Press the key combination [Ctrl] [C] to copy the row.

12. Select the entire table header row.

13. Press the key combination [Ctrl] [V] to paste it.

14. Size the table header row to accommodate the new format.

15. Select Format>Breaks from the menu.

16. Clear the Break Header option and click OK. (This will remove the break headers from each break)

Folding Breaks

- Summary calculations must be placed in the footer of a report structure, because this is the summary context.
    - However, many times we are not interested in the detail rows of the calculation. Therefore, we can use the Fold function to fold (hide) the details.
    - Later, in the advance course, we will learn to use context calculations and thus eliminate the need for folding the details of a table.

Portfolio Name	Trans Year	Trans Quarter	Revenue/ Expense
Biotech	2000	3	-400,996
	2000	4	31,108
	2001	1	-119,552
	2001	2	273,348
	2001	3	296,519
Biotech		Sum:	79,426
		Average:	15,885
		Count:	5
DOW 30	2000	3	-2,578,025
	2000	4	-1,807,386
	2001	1	330,360
	2001	2	1,340,480
	2001	3	4,066,066
DOW 30		Sum:	1,351,453
		Average:	270,291
		Count:	5
		Sum:	1,430,879
		Average:	143,088
		Count:	10

Portfolio Name	Trans Year	Trans Quarter	Revenue/ Expense
Biotech		Sum:	79,426
		Average:	15,885
		Count:	5
DOW 30		Sum:	1,351,453
		Average:	270,291
		Count:	5
Report		Sum:	1,430,879
		Average:	143,088
		Count:	10

Folding breaks allows us to hide the detail rows in a break, thus only showing the summaries in the break footers and header.

1. Open Ex 04 02.rep.
2. Click on the Report to Fold report tab to activate it.
3. Click anywhere on the table.
4. Select *Format>Breaks…* from the menu.
5. Select the Fold option.
6. Click OK.

You can use the same procedure that we used in the latter half of the previous exercise to remove the duplicate header rows. If we are working in version 6.x, we will not normally have the duplicate break headers, since version 6.x only displays the table header by default.

Standard Break Format

- The Standard Report Styles dialog allows you to preformat the breaks in all of your new master detail documents.
    - Select *Tools>Standard Report Styles...*
    - Breaks consist of the breaks themselves, and the table elements, such as headers, footers and the body of the structure. You can preset the formats for all of these elements.

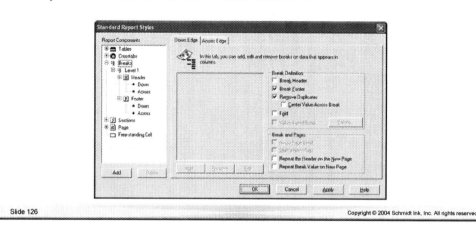

Breaks are very flexible and so are there formats. Some companies like the header repeated for each break, as in version 5.x, and some like only the table level header displayed, as in version 6.x. With the Standard Format Styles dialog, you can preset any break formats, except the new page behavior. (Not sure why this is not enabled)

126

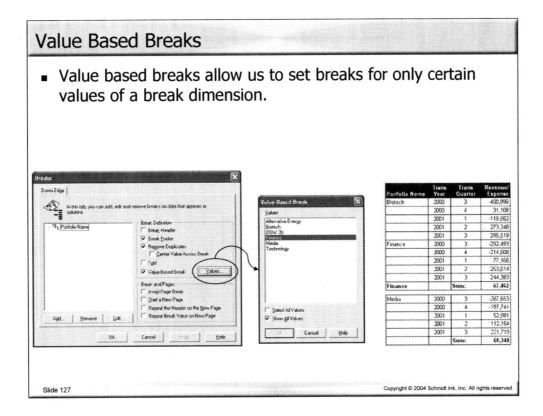

Value Based Breaks

- Value based breaks allow us to set breaks for only certain values of a break dimension.

The Value Based Break gives us an opportunity to set a break on a selected dimension values.

1. Click on the Value Based Break report tab to activate it.
2. Click anywhere on the table to select it.
3. Select *Format>Breaks…* from the menu.
4. Click the Add… button in the Breaks dialog.
5. Select Portfolio name and click OK.
6. Select the Value-Based Break option and click the Values… button.
7. Select DOW 30 and click OK.
8. Click OK in the Breaks dialog.
9. Click on any Revenue/Expense value and click the Insert Sum button.

The Insert Sum placed a total at the bottom of the table that totals all Revenue/Expense in the table. It also added a total in the DOW 30 break footer that only sums DOW 30 revenue/expense. This type of report may be misleading, because it looks as though the DOW 30 footer may be totaling all values above it and not just the DOW 30 values.

- BusinessObjects gives us the following options for page breaks within our break reports
  - Avoid Page Break: A break will start on a new page, if there is not enough for it to fit on the current page.
  - Start on a New Page: Each break will start on a new page.
  - Repeat the header on the New Page: If a break is interrupted by a new page, then the header will be repeated.
  - Repeat Break Value on New Page: If the duplicate values of a break have been removed, then the value will be repeated, if the break is interrupted by a new page.

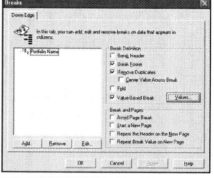

The page break formats only apply to printed reports or reports viewed in Page Layout mode.

1. Click on the Page Breaks report tab to activate it.

2. Select View>Page layout from the menu.

3. Scroll down to the bottom of page one and notice that the break body is intersected by the page break.

4. Click anywhere on the table to select it.

5. Select *Format>Breaks...* from the menu.

6. Select Portfolio Name in the breaks list.

7. Select the Avoid Page Break option.

8. Click OK. (Notice that the break that was intersected now starts on a new page)

128

First Level Course for BusinessObjects Reporter

Drilling into Reports

Data Drilling

- Drilling allows us to explore the details behind a summary report.
- There are basically three methods of drilling and each has its advantages, we will discuss all three.

Data Hierarchies

- Hierarchies are lists where the entities are arranged from most general to most specific, most powerful to most weakest, from the fewest to the most, and so forth.
    - We often think of hierarchies as pyramids. The most specific on top and the most general on the bottom.
- Every company has some sort of hierarchy
    - Decade>Year>Quarter>Week>Date
    - CEO>Directors>Middle Management>Analysts
    - Region>Country>State>City
    - Industry>Company>Product
- In all of the above examples, the entry on the left acts as a container for the entry on the right.
    - Decades contain Years
    - Years contain Quarters

Data Drilling

- Data drilling allows us to view reports in their most general (summarized) state. Then, when we want more detailed information, we drill into the hierarchy dimension.

- In the example below, we drilled into the year 2001. Then we drilled into the second quarter of 2001. In SI Equity, we can continue to drill all the way down to the dates in the hierarchy.

Trans Year	Revenue/ Expense
2000	-6,933,784
2001	8,510,980
Sum:	1,577,196

2001

Trans Quarter	Revenue/ Expense
1	349,438
2	2,750,713
3	5,410,828
Sum:	8,510,980

2001 - 2

Month Name	Revenue/ Expense
Apr	113,306
Jun	-287,497
May	2,924,905
Sum:	2,750,713

Different Methods of Drilling

- Drilling in BusinessObjects has evolved with the product. Therefore, there are different ways to perform drilling in a document.
    - You can define the depth of each hierarchy when you refresh the document. This will bring in all of the necessary information needed to perform a drill, which means that your document may be very large.
    - You can retrieve the next level of a hierarchy after the document has been refreshed. This will cause the entire query to be ran, which will include the entire set of data, plus the next level in the hierarchy.
    - You can redefine the scope of the hierarchy each time you drill. This will allow you to set conditions that will remove unnecessary data from your document, which will greatly improve query refresh times and document performance.
- We will discuss the last of these methods first, as it is probably the most efficient.

- **To use Scope of Analysis**
  -  Set the report into Drill mode by clicking the Drill toolbar button.
    - Right-click on a dimension value of interest and select Scope of Analysis.
      - In our case, right-click on Trans Year equal to 2001.
      - Notice that the dialog displays all of the hierarchies that are available in the report.
    - Select the objects in the hierarchy that you want to drill to.
      - In our case, we will select Trans Quarter.
    - Notice that there is a condition that will limit the data returned to the value that we right-clicked on.
      - In our case, select it to limit the data returned to the year 2001. Selecting this condition can greatly improve document performance.
    - Click OK

The Scope of Analysis drilling method is probably the most efficient method, because it allows us to set drill filters that limit the data in the document as we drill. The disadvantage is that it must requery the data source with each drill.

- After the OK button is clicked, the query will run with the new Trans Year equal to 2001. It will also return the quarters for that year.
- Place the cursor over a Trans Year value and it will turn into a magnifying glass. A tool tip may also pop-up and notify you of the next level. Double-click and the column will be repopulated with the next level in the hierarchy.
  - In our case, this is Trans Quarter.

Portfolio Industry	Trans Year	Revenue/ Expense	Num Transactions	Number Shares
Airlines	2001	73,700	29	-1,000
Alternative Energy	2001	303,886	96	-10,300
Automotive	2001	305,089	27	-4,400
Biotechnology	2001	904,852	139	-15,400
Chemical	2001	174,869	41	-2,300
Consumer	2001 Trans Quarter		194	-16,400
Finance	2001	1,011,943	148	-17,100
Industrial	2001	1,066,443	145	-11,900
Media	2001	487,116	81	-13,000
Metals	2001	432,050	32	-9,400
Oil and Gas	2001	408,532	33	-4,500
Technology	2001	2,333,168	454	-43,500
Telecom	2001	172,328	54	-8,800
Sum:		8,510,980	1,455	-155,900

2001

Portfolio Industry	Trans Quarter	Revenue/ Expense	Num Transactions	Number Shares
Airlines	1	-48,725	13	1,100
Airlines	2	67,738	13	-1,100
Airlines	3	54,688	3	-1,000
...		...		...
Technology	1	662,652	194	-3,200
Technology	2	280,281	197	-1,100
Technology	3	1,390,223	63	-39,200
Telecom	1	29,388	25	-2,700
Telecom	2	-180,088	23	4,800
Telecom	3	303,026	6	-8,500
Sum:		8,510,980	1,455	-155,900

1. Open Ex 05 01.rep.
2. Click on the Report to Drill report tab to activate it.
3. Select *Analysis>Drill* from the menu. (In most installations this will create a new report that we can drill into)
4. Right-click on the year 2001 and select *Scope of Analysis...* from the menu.
5. Select the filter Trans Year = 2001.
6. Select Trans Quarter.
7. Click OK.
8. Move your cursor over the value 2001 in the Trans Year column. (Your cursor should change into a magnifying glass)
9. Double-click to drill into the Trans Year.
10. Select Insert>Special Field>Drill Filters from the menu.
11. Click on the report, above the table, where you want to place the upper-left corner of the drill filter cell. (This will display the drill value on the report.)

Drilling with Drill Through

- Drill through allows you to drill through to any level of any available hierarchy. To drill through

  - 🔍 Set the document in Drill mode by clicking the Drill button.
    - Right-click on the dimension value in the report that you want to drill through and select *Drill Through...* from the pop-up menu.
    - Select the level that you want to drill to.
    - Click OK
    - The newly selected dimension will replace the original dimension in the table. Thus, we have drillrd through to the selected level.
- After the OK button is clicked, then the query will refresh with the entire data set, including the newly selected level.
  - This means that if we drilled through year 2001, as in the previous example, then the report will still contain data for both 2000 and 2001.

1. Open Ex 05 02.rep.
2. Click on the Report to Drill report tab to activate it.
3. Select *Analysis>Drill* from the menu.
4. Right-click on the year 2001 and select *Drill Through...* from the menu. (Notice that this dialog is very similar to the Scope of Analysis dialog in the previous example. However, it does not allow you to select a drill filter)
5. Select Trans Quarter.
6. Click OK. (This will retrieve the quarter information by adding Trans Quarter to the data provider and refreshing it. Then the Trans Year column will be replaced by the Trans Quarter column.)
7. Select Insert>Special Field>Drill Filters from the menu.
8. Click on the report, above the table, where you want to place the upper-left corner of the drill filter cell. (This will display the drill value on the report.)

- With this method, we define the scope of analysis in the Query Panel.
    - Click the Edit Data Provider button to open the Query Panel.
    - Click the Scope of Analysis button to display the available hierarchies.
    - Select the levels in the hierarchies that you expect to drill down to.
- Click the OK button and then Run.
    - This method differs from the previous scope of analysis method, because you are not able to select drill filters. This means that the query may return a large amount of data.

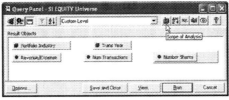

- **When the query has finished, then**
  - 🔍 Click the Drill button to place the report in Drill mode
    - Place your cursor over an interesting hierarchical dimension value
    - Double-click to drill into the dimension value

Portfolio Industry	Trans Year	Revenue/ Expense	Num Transactions	Number Shares
Airlines	2000	-4,325	25	1,000
Airlines	2001	73,200	29	-1,000
Alternative Energy	2000		78	10,200
Alternative Energy	2001	303,886	96	-10,200
Automotive	2000	-211,100	21	4,400
Automotive	2001	305,099	27	-4,400
Sum:		**378,039**	**276**	**0**

2001

Portfolio Industry	Trans Quarter	Revenue/ Expense	Num Transactions	Number Shares
Airlines	1	-48,725	13	1,100
Airlines	2	57,738	13	-1,100
Airlines	3	54,688	3	-1,000
Alternative Energy	1	14,341	49	1,300
Alternative Energy	2	226,017	36	-7,800
Alternative Energy	3	61,529	11	-3,700
Automotive	1	53,738	13	-1,000
Automotive	2	-34,613	11	900
Automotive	3	285,974	3	-4,300
Sum:		**682,685**	**152**	**-15,600**

1. Open Ex 05 03.rep.
2. Select *Data>Edit Data Provider...* from the menu.
3. Click the Scope of Analysis toolbar button in the Panel.
4. Select the Trans Quarter object in the list.
5. Click OK.
6. Click Run.
7. Select *Analysis>Drill* from the menu.
8. Move your cursor over the value 2001 in the Trans Year column. (Your cursor should change into a magnifying glass)
9. Double-click to drill into the Trans Year.
10. Select Insert>Special Field>Drill Filters from the menu.
11. Click on the report, above the table, where you want to place the upper-left corner of the drill filter cell.

- When a dimension value is drilled into, the value becomes a drill filter for the report.
    - For example, in the previous example, we drilled into year 2001. 2001, became a filter for the report, as shown below.
- To display drill filters (drill paths) on the report
    - Select Insert>Special Field>Drill Filters.
    - Click on the report where you want to place the upper-left corner of the special field.

2001				
Portfolio Industry	Trans Quarter	Revenue/ Expense	Num Transactions	Number Shares
Airlines	1	-48,725	13	1,100
Airlines	2	87,738	13	-1,100
Airlines	3	54,688	3	-1,000
Alternative Energy	1	14,341	49	1,300
Alternative Energy	2	228,017	36	-7,800
Alternative Energy	3	61,529	11	-3,700
Automotive	1	53,738	13	-1,000
Automotive	2	-34,613	11	900
Automotive	3	285,974	3	-4,300
	Sum:	682,685	152	-15,600

In the previous exercises, we used the Insert>Special Field>Drill Filters menu command to insert a cell into the report that will display the value drilled into. When a value is drilled into, BusinessObjects places a filter on the report that limits information to only the value drilled into. This special field shows all of the drilled into values, in the order that they were drilled into. This allows you to determine the Drill Path.

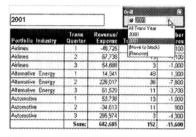
Many times after we have drilled into a value, we may want to see the report at the same level, but filtered by a different value. In MS Excel, this is known as a page filter.

As we drill into a report, BusinessObjects places a toolbar that displays the value that has been drilled into. The value is displayed in a drop down list that gives us several options. One of these options is the other dimension values. If we select one of these values, we will drill across the dimension.

1. In the drill report from the previous example, select the Trans Year value 2001, in the Drill toolbar drop-down list.

2. Now Select all All Trans Year. (This option will allow you to see the report as if there is no filter placed on the report. The danger here is that there is no longer any year dimension in the table. Therefore all quarters will merge, even if they are from different years)

3. Select Move to Block. (This option again removes the effects of the drill filter. However, there is no control as to where the column will be inserted into the table)

- Drilling up allows us to drill back up a hierarchy. To drill up
    - Right-click on the hierarchical dimension.
    - Select *Drill Up* from the menu.
    - This will replace the current hierarchical dimension with the next higher in the hierarchy, as shown below.
    - If you set drill filters, be sure to return to the Scope of Analysis to remove them.

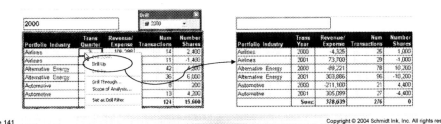

1. Click the Report to Drill report tab to activate it.
2. Click the Drill toolbar button.
3. Double-click on the Trans Year 2001.
4. Right-Click on a Trans Quarter value and select Drill up.

If you have not closed Ex 05 01.rep do the following

1. Select Window>Ex 05 01.rep from the menu.
2. Right-click on the table and select Scope of Analysis…
3. Clear the Trans Year = 2001 option and Click OK.
4. Right-click on any Trans Quarter value and select Drill Up.

If you used the filter option in the Scope of Analysis dialog and then wanted to drill up, you will probably have to revisit the dialog to remove the filter. This will cause the query to re-run and bring back a larger set of data.

Custom Hierarchies

- We can use the Hierarchy Editor to create custom hierarchies. We can
  - Rearrange existing hierarchies.
  - Create new hierarchies.
  - Add elements to existing hierarchies.
- The editor allows you to create hierarchies from non-universe sources, such as Microsoft Excel.

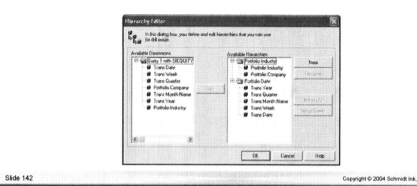

Sometimes, we do not have any hierarchies available. For example, when retrieving data from a text file.

1. Open Ex 05 04.rep. (This report was created from a personal data file with no hierarchical information)
2. Select *Analysis>Hierarchies...* from the menu.
3. Open the folder in the Available Dimensions section to make all of the dimensions visible.
4. Click the New button and name the new folder: Trans Date.
5. Double-click Trans Year, Trans Quarter, Trans Month, Trans Week, and Trans Date respectively. (This will place these objects in our new Trans Date hierarchy in the selected order)
6. Click OK.
7. Click the Drill toolbar button.
8. Double-click on a year value.
9. Double-Click on a quarter value.
10. Double-click on a month value.
11. Double-click on a week value.
12. Right-click and drill up.

142

First Level Course for BusinessObjects Reporter

Creating Queries

Introduction

- So far, we have worked with documents that were already created. In this section, we are going to discuss how to create queries.
- BusinessObjects will usually create some sort of default report when a new document is created.

BusinessObjects Universes

- BusinessObjects universes are logical mappings of data in a database. The good news is users do not have to know this mapping, only the available objects.
- Users simply have to know which universe to choose to retrieve desired information for documents.

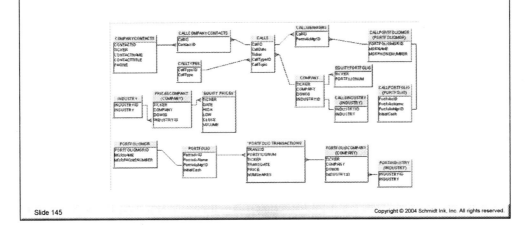

The good news is that we do not usually have to create the universes. This is usually done by specialists that understand how the data is related and how data is used. All we have to do is choose which universe we want to use in our documents.

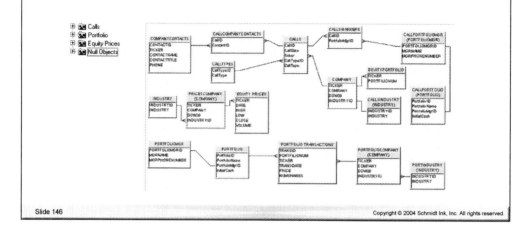
Contexts allow us to have more than one fact table in our universe. A fact table is a table that contains the transactions of a certain aspect of our business. For example, contact calls, marketing, sells, shipping, inventory, equity transactions, and so forth.

We usually can not directly relate two different fact tables, because the relationship may cause double-counting (which is generic for multiplying the results of any measures). Therefore, in order to have two different fact tables (different aspects of our business) in our universe, we create contexts to help us distinguish them.

In SI Equity, we have three contexts:

- Calls: This context contains all of the meeting information in our universe. It allows us to get information on any meetings that our portfolio managers had with our clients.

- Portfolio: This context allows us to get all of the information on our portfolios and the transactions that each has made.

- Equity Prices: This is for the prices history of every equity (stock) in our different portfolios.

Unfortunately, we usually can not create queries using objects from both contexts. For example, we can not create a simple query that returns objects from both Calls and Portfolio. As we become more advanced BusinessObjects users, we will learn how to use these different contexts to create more complex queries.

Building a New Document (New Report Wizard)

- To create a new document
  - Select *File>New...* from the menu to open the New Report Wizard.
    - Select Generate Standard Report to create a default report.
    - Select a template to create a report from a template.
    - Click Begin >
  - The next step allows you to select the type of data source
    - Choose Universe to use a universe.
    - Choose Other to use one of the many other data source types.

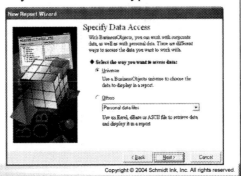

The New Report Wizard walks us through creating a new data provider for our document.

1. Select *File>New...* from the menu.
2. Leave Generate a Standard Report selected.
3. Click Begin>
4. Leave Universe selected.
5. Click Next>

Building a New Document (Query Panel)

- The next step allows you to select a universe.
    - If you plan on using the same universe for most of your documents, then you may want to select *Set as My Default Universe*.
    - Click Finish.
- If you have chosen a universe as your data provider, then the Query Panel will be displayed.
    - The Query Panel allows us to create queries on BusinessObjects universes.

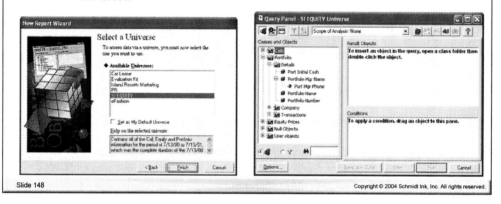

We use the Query Panel to create data providers from our universes. Other interfaces are used to create queries from different data provider types.

1. From the list of Available Universes, select SI Equity. (This list contains all of the universes that you have access to. There may be more, so if you do not see one that you may need, contact your BusinessObjects Supervisor and request access)

2. Click Finish (This will display the Query Panel)

Query Panel Data Types

Class
- Used to organize objects by category or group.

Dimension Object
- Usually identify information, such as Client ID's, stock ticker symbols, and locations. Since, dimensions identify information, they are used to synchronize data providers, define sections in Master-Detail reports, and define rankings in a report.

Detail Object
- Usually describe some attribute of a dimension. They usually contain information , such as weight, phone numbers, employee names, and so forth.

Measure Objects
- Usually are aggregates that conform to the dimensions in a report. They will usually sum, count, min, max, or average numerical information to a context defined by dimension values.

It is important to know what the different data provider object types represent and how they will behave in our reports. As we become more advanced, knowledge of these different types will allow us to create more and more powerful reports.

Classes and Objects Window

- The Classes and Objects window of the Query Panel contains all of the objects that are available in a universe.
- To open a class and expose the objects.
  - Click on the plus (+) sign preceding the class.
  - Or, Double-click on the class.
- Details are associated with Dimension objects.
  - If a Dimension object is preceded with a plus (+) there is a Detail associated with it.
  - Details usually have a one-to-one relationship with their parent dimension.
    - This means that for each dimension value, there should only be one detail value.

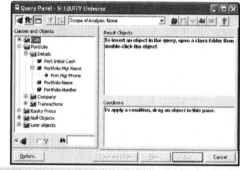

150

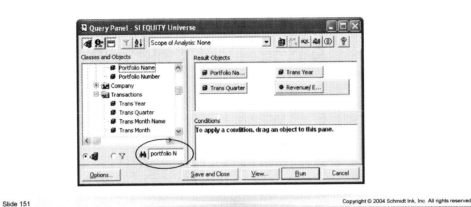
Version 6.x has a new search feature that allows you to type in a partial object name to find it in the panel.

1. Type Portfolio Name into the Search field. (As you type, notice that BusinessObjects will locate matching object names in the Classes and Objects window.)

Resizing the Query Panel

- Most of the borders of the Query Panel can be resized. Including the objects in the Result Objects and Conditions windows.

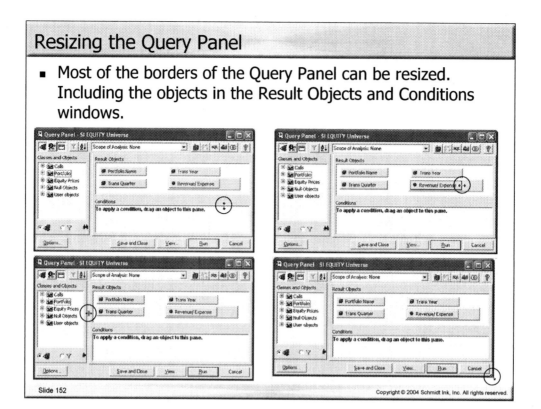

Resizing the Query Panel and it's objects allows us to adjust the panel to the size of our queries.

152

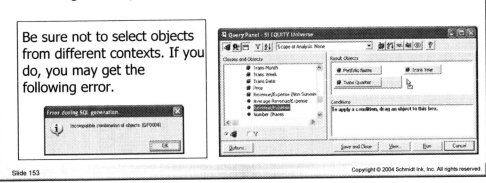

Selecting Objects for your Query

- To create a query, we simply place objects from the Classes and Objects window into the Result Objects window. To place objects in the Result Objects window, we can
  - Double-click objects in the Classes and Objects window.
  - Drag and drop objects into the window.
    - When dragging objects, they will be placed preceding the object that they are dropped on.
  - Drag and drop entire classes into the window.

Be sure not to select objects from different contexts. If you do, you may get the following error.

Objects placed in the Result Objects section will define the data set that is to be retrieved by the query.

1. Open the Portfolio Class in the Query Panel.
2. Open the Details folder.
3. Drag the Portfolio Name object to the Result Objects window.
4. Open the Company folder.
5. Double-click on the Portfolio Company object.
6. Open the Transactions folder.
7. Double-click on Trans Year and Revenue/Expense.

153

Running the Query

- The following five events happen when queries are ran
    - The query is first analyzed. At this point the query may be terminated by pressing the [Esc] button.

    | Press Esc to Cancel | Analyzing... | Time: | 0 | | 600 | |

    - Then the query is sent to the database, at this point the query, in many databases, can not be cancelled and the status bar may appear to be frozen.

    - When the database is through with the query, the rows are returned to the reporter, the user again cancel the operation.

    | | Updating data... | Time: | 3 | ▮▮▮▮ | 30 | |

    - Finally, the report is computed and formatted.

    | Report1: Computing data... | | | | |

    - The status bar displays the last execution date and time.

    | | Last Exec: 3/7/98 04:36 PM | | |

BusinessObjects must go through several phases before it can display a report in a document.

1. It must create SQL from the objects that you have selected. (SQL are the instructions that are sent to a database to retrieve a data set. We do not have to know how to create SQL, because BusinessObjects will do this for us)

2. We must wait for the database to collect the data. (This could be really quick or painfully slow. It all depends on the complexity of the query and the size of the data set)

3. The database must send the information to BusinessObjects. (During this phase BusinessObjects is just collecting the data)

4. Once all of the data is received, BusinessObjects must calculate all of the formulas in the report. Once this is done, it populates all of the cells in the report with the results. (This phase is usually relatively quick, but it can be slowed down by many complex calculations)

5. The execution time and date are displayed in the status bar.

- When a new document is created BusinessObjects uses the default template to create a report with all selected objects.
- The column headers are created from the object names.
  - To change a column header, double-click on the header and type in a new header.

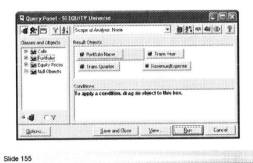

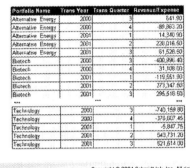

BusinessObjects uses the default report template to format the default report in a new document. This report can be found in the Template directory within the BusinessObjects 5.0 folder for version 5.x.

The default report is usually not that interesting, because it can not be very complex and anticipate every need. Probably the best templates just add a few cells, such as run date and if the report refreshed properly. Then the report can be manually formatted into any desired form.

1. Click the Run button.

Query Panel Functionality

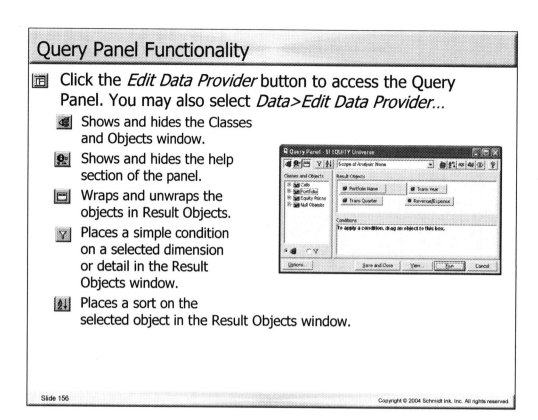

Click the *Edit Data Provider* button to access the Query Panel. You may also select *Data>Edit Data Provider...*

Shows and hides the Classes and Objects window.

Shows and hides the help section of the panel.

Wraps and unwraps the objects in Result Objects.

Places a simple condition on a selected dimension or detail in the Result Objects window.

Places a sort on the selected object in the Result Objects window.

This slide displays all of the toolbar buttons, and their functionality, on the left side of the dialog.

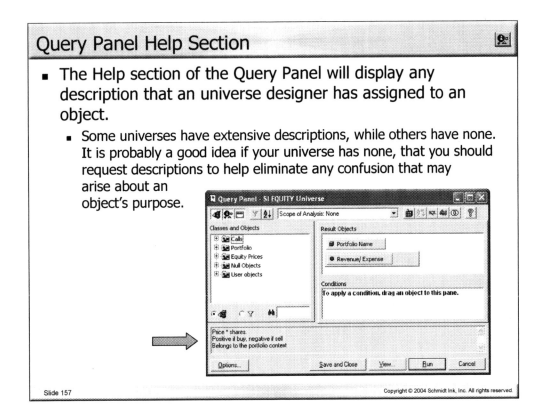

Query Panel Help Section

- The Help section of the Query Panel will display any description that an universe designer has assigned to an object.
  - Some universes have extensive descriptions, while others have none. It is probably a good idea if your universe has none, that you should request descriptions to help eliminate any confusion that may arise about an object's purpose.

The Help section can be very helpful when trying to determine the purpose for various objects in the panel. However, the universe designers must assign descriptions to the objects in order for there to be help text.

1. Select *Data>Edit Data Provider* from the menu.
2. Click the Show/Hide Help On Selected Item toolbar button.
3. Click on any object in the Classes and Objects window, or in the Result Objects window.

157

- Simple conditions allow us to select the values of a dimension or detail in our Result Objects window.
    - Select a dimension or detail in the Result Objects window.
    - Click the Simple Condition button.
    - Select the needed values from the list. Hold [Ctrl] or [Shift] key to select more than one value.
    - Click OK and a new condition will appear in the Conditions window.

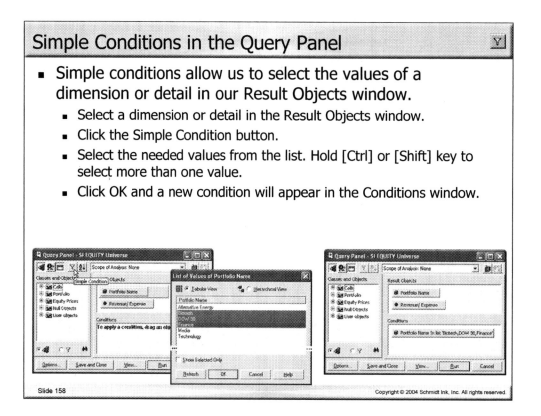

Slide 158

We can place simple conditions on dimensions in the Result Objects section of the panel.

1. Click the Portfolio Names object to select it.
2. Click the Simple Condition button.
3. Select some values in the list. (Hold the [Ctrl] to select multiple values)
4. Click OK to create the condition. (Look in the Conditions window and you will see your new condition)

158

- To apply a sort to an object in the Result Objects window
  - Select the object by clicking on it
  - Click the Sort toolbar button
    - To make the sort descending, double-click on the icon to change it's orientation.
- It is important to realize that the sort applied in the Query Panel applies to the data and not to any report structures.
  - BusinessObjects will only apply the sort to the report, if it is the first time the query has been ran.

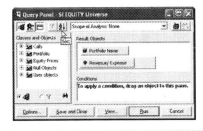 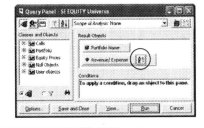

It is almost always unnecessary to place a sort in the Query Panel, because, as you have already learned, we usually place sorts directly to a report, via the Format Sorts dialog.

Sorts in the Query Panel cause our data set to be sorted before it is delivered to BusinessObjects. This may or may not allow BusinessObjects to compute a report faster.

1. Click on the Revenue/Expense object to select it.

2. Click on the Sort toolbar button. (This will place a sort icon directly on the Revenue/Expense object)

3. Double-click the sort icon on the Revenue/Expense object to change its orientation from ascending (A-Z) to descending (Z-A).

159

Viewing the SQL Generated by the Query Panel

- BusinessObjects creates instructions that instruct the data provider how to return data to a document. If the data provider is a relational database, then BusinessObjects will create SQL code.
  - SQL code helps us to understand how BusinessObjects is retrieving data.
  - We can make subtle changes to the SQL and then check the *Do not generate SQL before running* option.

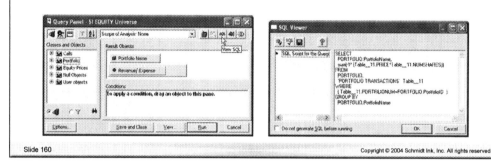

When first becoming familiar with a universe, it may be helpful to view the SQL generated by the Query Panel. If you do not understand SQL, don't worry, you will still be able to create reports. The SQL just helps you to understand)

1. Click on the View SQL button.
2. Click OK, when done viewing the SQL.

Query Options

- Query options allow us to set certain options on our queries
    - No Duplicate Rows: This option tells BusinessObjects not to retrieve redundant information. This option is usually only useful if the query contains no measure objects.
    - Partial Results: This allows us to limit the number of rows returned by a query. Useful for testing and for returning the top or bottom number of rows based on a measure in the query.
        - Top 10: Sort measure descending and set Partial Results to 10 Rows.
    - Do Not Retrieve Data: This option purges the query of any data, but saves the query structure.

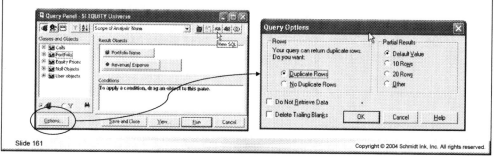

The Query Options allows us to place certain limits or actions on our queries. For example, when retrieving data that contains no measures, it is probably a good idea to select No Duplicate Rows.

1. Click the Options... button.
2. Select 20 Rows.
3. Click OK.

So far, we have placed a filter that limits the Portfolio Names returned, we have sorted the Revenue/Expense object in descending order, and we have limited the rows returned to 20 rows. When we run this query, it will return the top 20 Portfolio Name, Portfolio Company, Trans Year combinations based on Revenue/Expense.

4. Click Run

Data Manager

- BusinessObjects documents can contain one or more data providers, and each data provider can contain many objects.
- To manage all of this information, we use the Data Manager.
  - 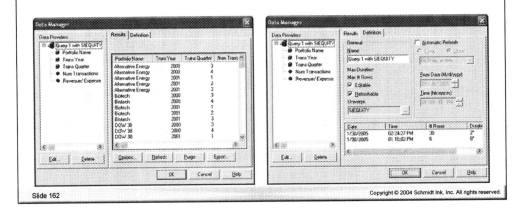 We open the manager by clicking on the View Data toolbar button, or by selecting *Data>View Data...* from the menu.
    - The Data Manager has two tabs – Results and Definition.

Notice the Edit and Delete buttons below the Data Providers section. The Edit button calls the Query Panel and the Delete button deletes queries from a report.

162

- The Results tab allows us to view the data in a data provider. It also allows us to
    - Refresh a signal provider
    - Purge the data from a signal data provider
    - Export the data to different formats
        - The Edit>Copy All and File>Save As menu options also allow us to export reports in a document. The export option, exports the data of a data provider.

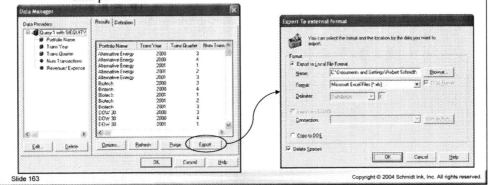

Slide 163

Notice that in this example, there is a yellow partial results warning icon. The data provider returned partial results, because we limited the query to 20 rows. You can also get partial results for other reasons, probably the most common reason is a limit set by the Universe Designer. The default number of rows returned by a universe is 5000.

1. Click the View Data toolbar button.
2. Examine the Results tab. (It list all of the data returned in the data section. It also has four buttons that allow you to work with the data set)

163

Data Manager - Definition Tab

- The Definition tabs allows us to
  - Name the Data Provider.
  - Set Edit and Refresh permissions.
  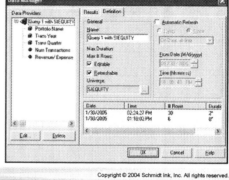 Change the universe used by the Query Panel. The universe must have the same objects in order to replace an existing universe.
  - Set Automatic Refresh options. The document must be opened during the scheduled time in order to refresh.
  - View Query Statistics
    - Date
    - Time
    - Number of Rows
    - Duration
      " = seconds
      ' = minutes

1. Click on the Definition tab to activate it.

2. Enter a new data provider name into the Name field. We can call it top 20. (This will rename our data provider)

3. Have a look at the query times, number of rows and the duration of each refresh. (These times should not vary too much, unless the query was modified. If they do, you need to ask your database administrator why the query times vary so much)

164

Alternate Data Providers

- There are several alternate types of data providers and they are available in different combinations for different companies.
    - Freehand SQL: allows SQL to be entered directly.
    - Personal Data Provider: allows us to use text files, MS Excel documents, and other flat file types.
    - Stored Procedures: Predefined data sources that are optimized (hopefully) to return complex data.
    - VBA: Uses a record set defined in VBA. This method is for developers and is very similar to Stored Procedures.
    - XML: Uses a XML data source.

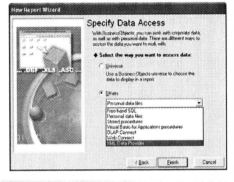

Universes are created mostly for relational databases, such as Oracle, SQL Server, MS Access, etc. However, there are different kinds of data sources other than these databases, such as flat files, MS Excel, OLAP data sources, and so forth. Alternate Data Providers allow us to access these types of data sources.

There are also times where we may want to access a relational database through our own code and not through a universe. Stored procedures and freehand SQL allow us to do this. BusinessObjects does not check these two methods, so when you use them the writer must take responsibility.

165

- Select Personal data files in the New Report Wizard
  - This will cause the Access Personal Data dialog to be displayed.
- In the Access Personal Data dialog
  - Select the format of the data – Text files, MS Excel, ...
  - Click the Browse... button and find the data file
  - If the data file has column headers, click the First Row Contains Column Names option.

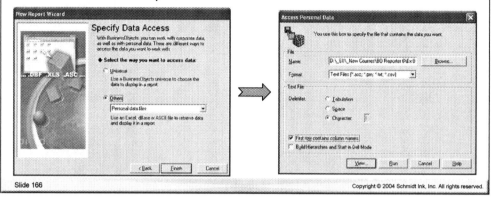

In this example, we will use a text file has a data source. Many companies do this sooner or later, because they may receive data in a file format, but not have the ability to import the file into a database (warehouse).

1. Select *File>New...* from the menu.
2. Select Generate a Standard Report and click Begin>
3. Select the Others option and then Personal data files in the drop list.
4. Click Finish.
5. Select Text Files in the Format dropdown list.
6. Select the First Row Contains Header Names option.
7. Click the Browse... button.
8. Locate and select Ex 05 04.rep.
9. Click the Open button.
10. Click the Run button.

- BusinessObjects will type all text values as dimensions and all numeric values as measures.
  - Not all numeric values are measures – Employee ID's, Zip codes, …
- To retype a measure as a dimension
  - Open the Data Manager.
  - Select the object in the Data Providers list.
  - Click on the Definition tab.
  - Select the correct qualification in the Qualification section of the dialog.

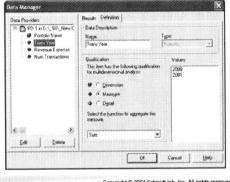

In the previous slide, we imported a text file into our document. However, there is a problem – BusinessObjects has assumed that all numeric fields are measures. This is not always the case. For example, years are not measures and neither are quarter numbers.

We use the Data Manager to re-qualify these mistakenly assigned object qualifications.

1. Select *Data>View Data…* from the menu.
2. Click on the Definition tab to activate it.
3. Click on the Trans Year object in the Data Providers section. (Notice that it is qualified as a measure)
4. Select the Dimension qualification.
5. Repeat steps 3 and 4, for Trans Quarter, Trans Month and Trans Week.
6. Click OK to dismiss the Data Manager.

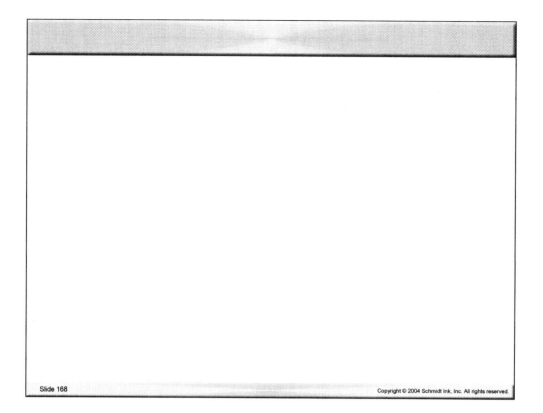

First Level Course for BusinessObjects Reporter

Conditions in Queries

169

- Conditions on queries allow users to retrieve only the information of interest from a database.
  - For example, a database may contain information for many different years or products. Conditions allow constraints to limit the information retrieved to selected years or products.
- Since conditions limit data in a document, the right combination of conditions can make documents more efficient and responsive.

When users forget to place conditions on queries, they may resort to extreme measures to express their displeasure.

Conditions allow us to retrieve only data of interest from a database, which makes our queries more efficient and compact. We should carefully consider each condition and make sure it is doing exactly what we need it to do. For example, some companies fiscal year is not the same as a calendar year. Therefore, it is important for them to use a fiscal year condition to retrieve data for a certain year.

If we did not have conditions, we would have to bring the entire data set to our document and then filter the data to show only what interests us. This would make are documents awkward and difficult to work with. This example is an extreme, but it does illustrate the importance of conditions in your query.

As we get more advanced, we will learn more and more creative ways to place conditions on our queries. We will not cover all of these methods, but it is important to realize that there are many creative ways to create conditions to get exactly what we need from our data provider.

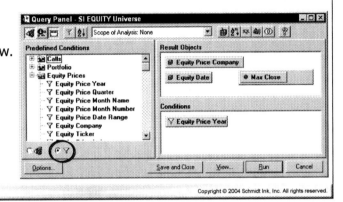
When universe designers create universes, they not only create dimensions, details, and measures, they also should create conditions that we can quickly and confidently place on our queries.

1. Select *File>New...* from the menu.

2. Select the SI Equity universe as the data provider.

3. Click on the Condition option below the Classes and Objects window.

4. Open the folders in the Predefined Conditions window. (The Classes and Objects window changes into the Predefined Conditions window, when you select the Condition option.)

5. Double click on Equity Price Year in the Equity Prices class. (It will then be placed in the Conditions section of the Panel.)

The condition that we have selected in this example will prompt us for a year value, when the query is refreshed. Not all conditions prompt for values.

171

- Universe Designers often provide pre-defined conditions that can be used to limit data.

  - When combining two or more conditions on the same object, the conditions must be Or'ed together. This example reads - The year can either be 2001 or 2000.

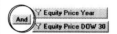

  - When combining two or more conditions on the different objects, the conditions should be And'ed together. This example reads – A row of data must contain the Equity Price Year and DOW 30.

    Note: Double-click on the logic icon (And, Or) to toggle it from And to Or to And...

Most queries contain more than one condition. Therefore, we must know how to combine them to logically return the data of interest. BusinessObjects supplies us with two logical operators to combine conditions – And & Or.

The And states that two object conditions on the same row should be true in order to return the row. The Or could state that one of two object conditions on the same row should be true. It also states that a single object should be one of several values to return a row.

1. Remove any conditions in the Panel.

2. Double-click Call Year 2000 and Call Year 2001. (They both will be placed in the Conditions window. Notice that they are probably And'ed together. Since the condition is placed on the same object, this combination can never be true. A year can never be equal to two values.)

3. Double-click on the And operator to change it to an Or operator. (Now the condition combination will return data if any Call Year equals 2000 or 2001)

- Many times we need conditions that combine And and Or logic. When combining logic, the And operator has precedence over the Or operator.

- In this case, we want the Dow 30 equities for Year 2001 or for Year 2000.

- Operator's within parenthesis are combined first. Parenthesis are created by right clicking on the operator and selecting Shift Right from the pop-up menu.

- In this case, we want the same as the above condition – Dow 30 Equities for Year 2001 or for Year 2000.

Now that we know that we can only use And & Or logic to create conditions on our queries, we have to learn how to use them efficiently.

1. Clear any conditions from the Conditions section of the Query Panel.

2. Double-click Call Year 2001, Call DOW 30, Call Year 2000, and Call DOW 30. (Notice that we have the same condition twice (Call DOW 30) in our logical statement. This is something that we are not allowed to do in the Result Objects window.)

3. Right-click on the first logical operator (And or Or, it could be either) and select Shift Right. (This is how we create parentheses to group the priorities within our logical statement)

4. Right-click on the third operator and shift it right.

5. The two shifted right operators should be And's & the outer operator should be an Or. Double-click on the operators until this is true. (This type of configuration states that either set of the And'ed conditions could be true in order to return a row.)

173

Custom Conditions

- Simple conditions and designer conditions work well in many cases, but sometimes we need to create a condition.
- Custom conditions allow us to
  - Use the different logical operators that are available.
  - Use the different types of operands in BusinessObjects.
  - Create conditions that the designer did not supply us with.

The Designers can create many conditions, but they probably can not anticipate every need for a condition in our documents. Therefore, BusinessObjects has allowed us to create our own custom conditions.

174

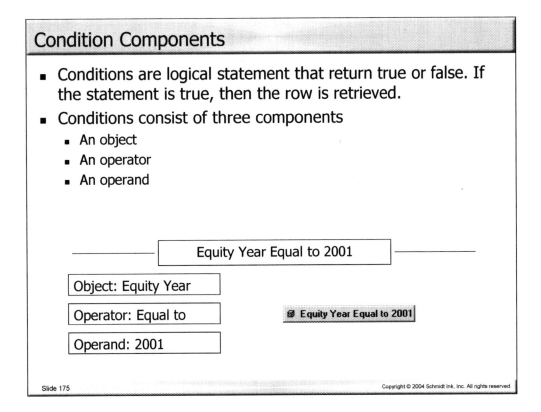

Most conditions contain three different components. An object, an operator, and an operand.

- Select the object for a condition by dragging it from the Classes and Objects window into the Conditions window.
  - Almost any object can be used in a condition. Although, the universe designer may not allow certain objects, because they will slow query performance too drastically.
    - For example, you may not be allowed to place a condition on a large text field.

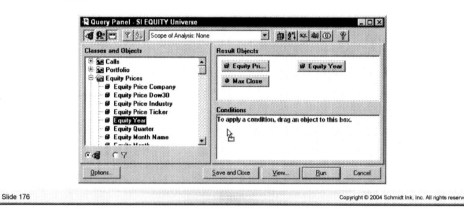

To select an object for a condition, we simply drag it from the Classes and Objects window and drop it into the Conditions window. In the beginning, you may be tempted to drag it from the Result Objects window, but this is not allowed.

1. Drag Equity Year into the Conditions window.

Selecting an Operator

- After a user places an object in the Conditions window, the Classes and Objects window switches to the Operators window.
  - An operator is chosen by double-clicking on it.
- We will discuss the available operators in the following slides.
- The operator can be replaced at any time by first selecting the operator portion of the condition and then by double-clicking a new operator.

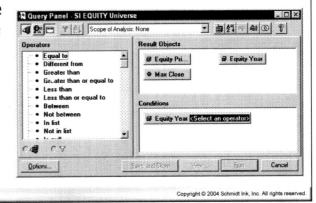

After you drag an object into the Conditions window, the operator part of the condition is highlighted and the Classes and Objects window changes into the Operators window.

You can change the Classes and Objects window to the Operators window at any time by selecting the operator part of a condition. This will also allow you to quickly change the operator portion of an existing condition.

1. Double-click on the Equals to operator.

177

Selecting an Operand Type

- BusinessObjects offers the following types of operands
  - Constant
  - List of Values
  - Prompt
  - List of Prompts
  - Another Object
  - A subquery
  - A calculation

- Users select operand types by double-clicking on them in the Operands window.
- The operand can be changed at any time by selecting the operand on the object in the Conditions window and choosing another from the Operands window.

When an operator is assigned to a condition, the Operators window changes to the Operands window. You can also change the Classes and Objects window into the Operands window at any time by selecting the operand portion of a condition.

1. Double-click Type a new constant in the Operands window.

We have now created a simple condition on the Equity Year object.

- The Equal to operator allows information to be returned when the object portion of the condition exactly matches the operand portion.
- In many systems this match includes the case of the word.
  - For example, CASE = CASE and CASE ≠ Case.
- The Different From operator allows information to be returned when the object portion of the condition does not exactly match the operand portion.
  - This is the same as Not Equal To.

The 'Equals to' operator returns rows when an object equals a certain value. This is the type of logic that we use most often. However, sometimes we are interested in retrieving rows when an object is not equal to a certain value. For example, *Revenue/Expense Different from 0*.

The different from operator allows us to eliminate unwanted information from our query. For example, suppose that a developer put a test account in our production warehouse. It would be quite annoying if this bogus account appeared in our corporate documents. If this is the case, we could place *Account Different from Bogus Account* and ignore this account in the universe.

- The range operators allow us to return information when the object value is greater than, less than or even between the operand value(s).
- Range operators work with numbers, dates or text. Below are some examples
    - Number Greater than 5
      Will return 6, 7, 8, …
    - Number less than or equal to 5
      Will return …, -1, 0, 1, 2, 3, 4, 5.
    - Name Greater than 'B'
      Will return Bertha, Betty, …
    - Name Between 'B' and 'C'
      Will return all names that start with B
    - Date Between 1/1/99 and 1/31/99
      Will return all data for January 1999

Range operators allow us to bring back information when a range of conditions are true. For example, *Revenue/Expense Greater than 100000.*

As shown above, the range operators also work on text values. Remember in college during registration? At my school they would divide the people up into groups defined by their last names.

Name Greater than 'A' And Name Less than 'F'

Or

Name Greater than or Equal to 'F' And Name Less Than 'Z'

Or

Name Greater than 'Z'

The last section would have had a very boring day, since it only defines names that begin with Z. Notice that I did not use the equal to portion of the operator on the Z section. This is because, I doubt if anyone's last name is simply Z.

Operator - Matches Pattern

- The Matches Pattern operator allows users to specify wild cards in their conditions.
- For example, if a user wanted to return all customers whose name started with a B, the user would use the following
    - Customer Matches Pattern 'B%'
    - The percent sign allows users to represent any number of unknown characters.
- Suppose a user wanted to know three letter names that start with a B and end with an R. The user would use the following
    - Customer Matches Pattern 'B_r'
    - The underscore allows users to represent one unknown character.

The Matches Pattern is a great operator that allows us to define wild cards for text conditions. For example, suppose we wanted all equities that started with the letter A. We could build a condition like, Equity Price Company Matches Pattern 'A%'.

The above example is relatively efficient and it will return all equities that start with the letter 'A'. Now suppose that we wanted to create a condition that returned all products that end with the pattern – '5AH'? We could do the following: Product Number Match Pattern '%5AH'. This query is not very efficient, because it can not use and index to locate the values.

An analogy to the above examples would be if I asked you the show me all of the words in a dictionary that started with the letter 'A'. Easy enough, you just show me those pages. However, if I asked you to show me all of the words that ended with 'ion', it would be near impossible. If you requested this from a database, it would take much longer than the former example.

Operator – Is Null / Is Not Null

- A Null is an unassigned value. This misses assignment can be explicit or implicit.
  - Explicit: The value was never assigned in the database. For example, in a contact management system you may leave the cell phone field empty.
  - Implicit: Supposed you chose the Customer and Invoice objects from a sales universe. The Customer object represents all of your customers and the invoice object represents all of you invoices, both are completely assigned. However, when you select both together, there may be customers with no invoices. These customers will have Null invoice numbers.
- The Is Null operator allows you to retrieve rows where an object's value is Null.
- The Is Not Null operator allows you to return rows where an object's value is not Null.

This is a very important operator, as it allows you to retrieve or ignore rows that have Null values. Null values are fields that have never been assigned a value.

- Users can enter a constant operand into the condition, by first double-clicking on the *Type a new constant* operand and then entering the value into the edit field on the condition.
  - Constants can also be entered by first double-clicking on the operand portion of the condition and then typing a constant value.
  - There is no need to enter quotes for text entries, as BusinessObjects will place quotes for text objects.

This is the version 6.x Query Panel. It contains a new operand – Select Query Results. This is a very powerful new operand that could greatly increase you ability to make flexible and efficient queries.

Now that we know all of the available operators, it is time to discuss the operands.

The first of the operands, and maybe the most common, is *Type a new constant*. This operand allows you to type in the value for the operand. It is quick and easy, but sometime also error prone. It is error prone, because you may mistype the value. For example, suppose the condition was on quarters in a year and you entered Q4. Seems reasonable, but maybe the quarters are not stored that way. Maybe they are stored like Qtr 4. These two values are not the same and no data would be retrieved.

Operand – Show List of Values

- *Show list of values* also allows us to enter a constant value for the operand. However, instead of typing the value, we are allowed to select it from a list.
  - Selecting values ensures that they will be of the same case and spelled the same. Therefore, eliminating human error.
  - The list may take significantly longer to display the first time it is used, because it must run a query to retrieve the values.

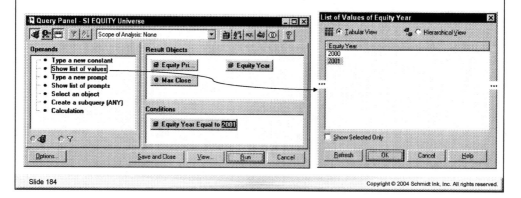

The list of values operand is very similar to the type a new constant operand, as both place constants in the operand. However, the list of values operand allows you to select a value or values from a list.

The only disadvantage of this type of operand is that the first time it is used for an object, BusinessObjects must run a query to return the values for the list. In some cases, this could take a relatively long time, in others not so bad. The good news is that once the list is created, it will not have to update, until you click the Refresh button in the List of Values dialog.

Not all objects have a list of values associated with them. For example, most measures do not have a list of values. Neither do large text fields.

Operand – Type a New Prompt

- The *Type a new prompt* operand prompts for input when the report is refreshed.
    - Values can then be entered by typing a constant value or by selecting a value from the list. Not all objects have lists associated with them. For example, measures usually do not, dates may not, and long text objects usually do not.
    - The prompts will sort alphabetically in the Enter or Select Values dialog.

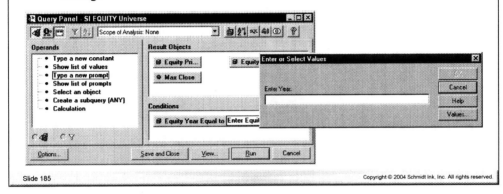

The prompt is an extremely flexible way to allow people to enter values for a condition, as the report is refreshed. They can type a new value, or in most cases, select a value from a list.

- Sometimes, we want to create queries that use the same prompts as other queries in our documents. For example
  - In a union query
  - When building a multiple data provider document.
- By using the same text in each prompt, we are able to create one prompt that supplies an operand value to multiple queries.
  - The list of prompts ensures that the prompts used in both queries are identical.

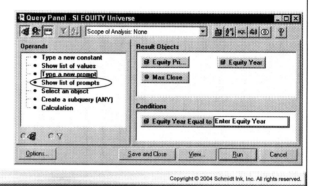

The show list of prompts is an efficient way to use the same prompt in different queries of the same report, or in different conditions in the same query.

If two queries in the same report contain the same prompt text, then the value will only be prompted for once when the document is refreshed. This allows us to use the same operand value in two different conditions. (If the prompt text differs by only one character, BusinessObjects will display both prompts when the document is refreshed)

Operand – Select an Object

- BusinessObjects allows other objects to be used as an operand. This allows the condition to equate the values of two different objects.
  - The outcome of this type of operand is often unpredictable, because it creates a relation with another object in the universe. Knowledge of the tables in the universe and their relations will help to eliminate unpredictable behavior.

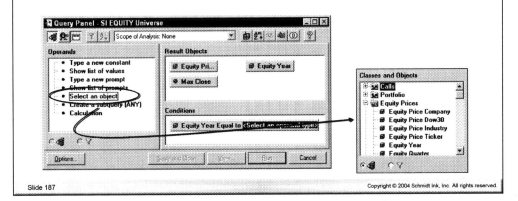

We can use other objects as an operand. Sometimes this is a good idea, sometimes it is not. The reasons why are too technical for the scope of this course, but it is important to realize, so that you always check the validity of a results returned when an object is used as an operand in a condition.

Okay, I will tell you why. Those of you that know SQL know that we join tables in a query by equating two fields in the different table. For example, Trans Year equal to Call Year. In most cases, the universe designer has carefully considered all joins in the universe and made all of the joins that will allow data to be safely retrieved. Now, when you create a condition equating one object to another, you just created a new join in the universe. Is it right? Could be....

When you become more advanced, you will learn to use subqueries. In most cases, you could use a subquery to get the results that you wanted by equating two objects.

Operand – Create a Subquery

- The In List operator allows you to enter a list of values for an operand. The Create a Subquery operand will dynamically create this list using a query on the universe.
  - There a many uses for this type of operand, and many of them are discussed in the advanced portion of this course.

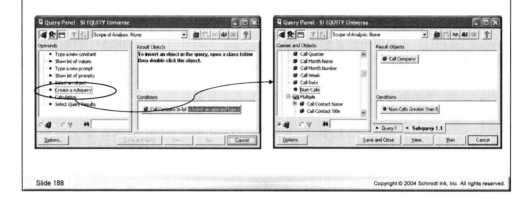

The subquery is a very powerful way to create many different kinds of queries. Probably the most common use is to build a list of values for the In List operator, as shown in the slide.

This topic is covered in much more detail in the advanced course from Schmidt Ink, Inc. (www.SchmidtInk.com)

Operand – Select Query Results (Version 6.x)

- This operand is very powerful and allows us to use an object's values from another data provider in the same document.
  - This means that we can now use lists in a MS Excel file, another universe, or and y other data source available.

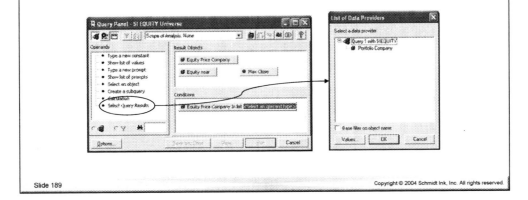

This is a great operand that is now available in BusinessObjects 6.x. It allows you to use other data providers to return a list for your condition.

This topic is covered in much more detail in the advanced course from Schmidt Ink, Inc. (www.SchmidtInk.com)

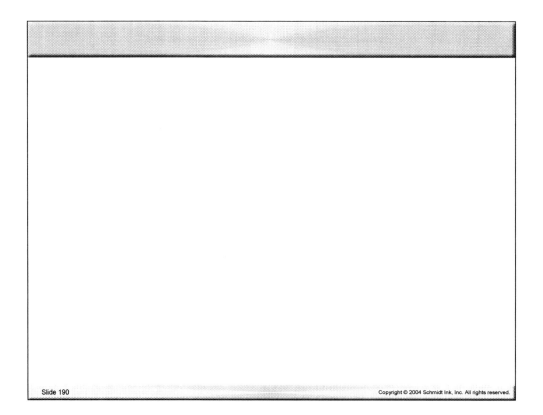

Advanced Course for BusinessObjects Reporter

Document Data

191

Introduction

- All documents contain data and all reports are a view of the data in a document.
- In this chapter, we are going to discuss the data sets that are found in documents.
  - We are going to discuss object behavior
  - Talk about multiple data sets
  - Discuss how to relate multiple sets of data in a document

192

Data Sets in Documents

- Documents can contain one of more sets of data
  - These sets are known as data providers
  - Data providers can come from different sources
    - Universes, Personal Data Providers, Stored Procedures, VBA, …
- The data providers may or may not be linked
  - Linked data providers are synchronized and logically related
  - Unlinked data providers are independent of one another

Portfolio Name
Portfolio Manager Name
Revenue/Expense

Data Provider #1

Call Portfolio Name
Num Calls

Data Provider #2

Portfolio Company
Revenue/Expense

Data Provider #3

Documents can contain one query, several queries, or even very many queries. The number of queries depends on the purpose of the reports that the document contains.

Documents with one set of data, or a single data provider, are less complex, because the chances of displaying erroneous information increase with the number of data providers in a document. This does not mean that multiple data provider documents are very difficult to create; it simply means that there are more considerations to make in multiple data provider documents.

193

Data Providers are Collections of Data Objects

- Data Objects are qualified as Dimensions, Details, or Measures
- Each object qualification has different characteristics.
  - Dimensions are usually identifying information, such as Client ID's, stock ticker symbols, and locations. Since, dimensions identify information, they are used to synchronize data providers, define sections in Master-Detail reports, and define rankings in a report.
  - Measures usually are aggregates that conform to the dimensions in a report. They will usually sum, count, min, max, or average numerical information to a context defined by dimension values.
  - Details usually describe some attribute of a dimension. They usually contain information information, such as weight, phone numbers, employee names, and so forth.
- Understanding how each of these objects behave in a report or document will greatly enhance our advanced reporting skills.

One of three data object types represents all data in a document. Each of these types has different behavior and significance in a document.

Universe designers assign the type to the data objects, so there is some room for errors on the part of the designers. In this course, we will assume that all measures are associated with an aggregate function and all details have a one-to-one relationship with their dimension parent.

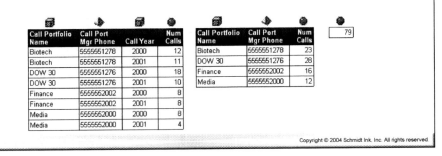

Object Behavior

- Follow the directions in the notes section of this slide
    - There is only one detail value per manager name. Therefore, the manager phone number is a detail of the manager
    - In the first table, the query returns the sum of calls for each manager.
        - Calculated when the query is executed
    - Then, after the Call Year column is deleted, the number of calls conform to the new context
        - Calculated in the report

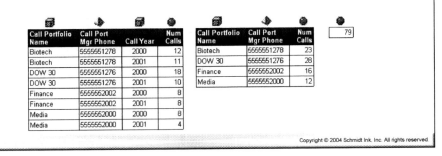

1. Create a new report using the SI Equity universe.

2. Select *Call Portfolio Name*, *Call Port Mgr Phone*, *Call Year*, and *Num Calls* from the Calls folder.

3. Click the Run button.

4. Select Edit->Duplicate Report from the menu.

5. Delete the Call Year column from the table.

6. Drag the Num Calls data from the table and drop it on the report. Hold down the [Ctrl] key before releasing the mouse.

7. Examine the results and then delete the duplicated report, thus leaving a report with the original table.

The *Call Port Mgr Phone* is an attribute of the *Call Port Mgr Name* dimension. Therefore, there must be only one value per portfolio. BusinessObjects assumes that there will only be one attribute value per dimension value.

The *Num Calls* measure contains two levels of aggregation. The first is in the database, where it instructed to return the number of calls for each combination of non-measure objects. E.g. the total for each row returned. The second level of aggregation instructs it to sum to any new context level in the report. This is why it re-aggregates when we delete a dimension column or place it alone on the report.

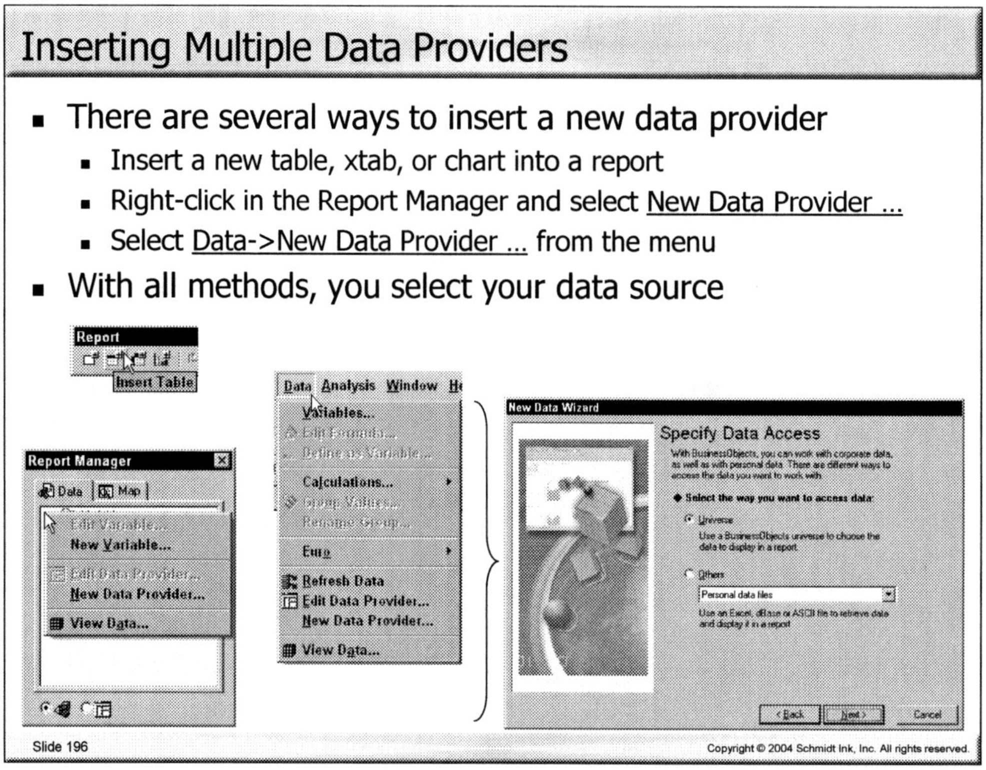

Inserting Multiple Data Providers

- There are several ways to insert a new data provider
  - Insert a new table, xtab, or chart into a report
  - Right-click in the Report Manager and select <u>New Data Provider ...</u>
  - Select <u>Data->New Data Provider ...</u> from the menu
- With all methods, you select your data source

Slide 196

There are several methods to inserting another data provider into a document, three of which are shown above.

Another data provider will import data that is not available in the first data provider. The additional data provider usually accesses data in another context of the same universe or a different data source altogether.

We may also bring data in from the same universe and context, but at different levels of aggregation. This is not always necessary, and if this is the case, one should consider using the original query for the document.

- Follow the directions in the notes section of this slide
    - This exercise will insert a completely independent data provider into our document. It will not be linked to the existing data provider, because it is from a completely different data source
    - Note that the Trans Year column is displaying one year for each Portfolio Name and that this year is 4001! It is doing this, because it thinks that the Trans Year object is a measure, and it is simply adding the two years – 2000 + 2001. To make it display properly, we will have to re-qualify it to a dimension.

Portfolio Name	Num Transactions	Revenue Expense	Trans Year
Alternative Energy	174.00	214,664.60	4,001.00
Biotech	184.00	79,425.70	4,001.00
DOW 30	1,491.00	1,351,453.00	4,001.00
Finance	120.00	67,462.30	4,001.00
Media	120.00	-78,540.30	4,001.00
Technology	591.00	-57,269.80	4,001.00

1. Open the file from the previous exercise: Ex 01.rep.
2. Select Insert->New Data Provider ... from the menu.
3. Click the Access new data in a different way option and click Begin.
4. Select the Others option and Personal Data Files from the drop list.
5. Click the Finish button.
6. Click the Browse button and locate the Ex 02.txt file in the Adv Doc Data folder. Then click Open.
7. Select the First row contains column names option.
8. Then click the Run button.
9. Click the By Data Provider option in the Report Manager.
10. Open the PD 2 folder and select all of the objects it contains.
11. Drag the objects onto the report to create a table.

- When using a data provider, other than an universe, BusinessObjects will often qualify
  - Text as dimension/character
  - Dates as either dimension/date or dimension/character
  - Numbers as measure/numeric
    - Not all numbers are measures – ID's, years, and so forth
- Re-qualify erroneous qualifications with the Data Manager

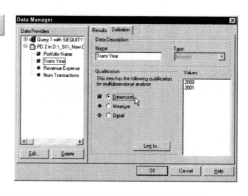

1. Select <u>Data->View Data...</u> from the menu.

2. Click the plus sign in front of the respective data provider in the list to expand the folder and reveal the objects.

3. Click the object in the Data Provider list that needs to be re-qualified. In this case the *Trans Year* object.

4. Activate the Definition tab, by clicking on it.

5. Make sure the name of the object is in the <u>Name</u> field, so that we are not re-qualifying the wrong object.

6. Select the <u>Dimension</u> option in the <u>Qualification</u> section.

7. Then click the OK button.

Notice the the dates on the table are now correct and that there are two dates for each portfolio – 2000 and 2001.

Portfolio Name	Num Transactions	Revenue Expense	Trans Year
Alternative Energy	78.00	-89,221.30	2,000.00
Alternative Energy	96.00	303,885.90	2,001.00
Biotech	91.00	-369,888.40	2,000.00
Biotech	93.00	449,314.10	2,001.00
DOW 30	675.00	-4,385,412.50	2,000.00
DOW 30	816.00	5,736,865.50	2,001.00
Finance	45.00	-507,100.70	2,000.00
Finance	75.00	574,563.00	2,001.00
Media	62.00	-465,393.90	2,000.00
Media	58.00	386,853.60	2,001.00
Technology	274.00	-1,116,767.25	2,000.00
Technology	317.00	1,059,497.45	2,001.00

- If the data from different data providers is to remain separate, then there is no reason to link them. However, if the data from both providers are to be included in the same table, xtab, chart, or formula, then they must be linked.
- In the example below, the Call Port Mgr Phone detail object is incompatible with the other table. Also notice, that the Num Calls column displays the same value in each cell.

Call Portfolio Name	Call Port Mgr Phone	Call Year	Num Calls
Biotech	5555551278	2000	12
Biotech	5555551278	2001	11
DOW 30	5555551276	2000	18
DOW 30	5555551276	2001	10
Finance	5555552002	2000	8
Finance	5555552002	2001	8
Media	5555552000	2000	8
Media	5555552000	2001	4

Portfolio Name		Trans Year	Num Transactions	Revenue Expense	Num Calls
Alternative Energy		2000	78.00	-89,221.30	79
Alternative Energy	⊘	2001	96.00	303,885.90	79
Biotech		2000	91.00	-369,888.40	79
Biotech		2001	93.00	449,314.10	79
DOW 30		2000	675.00	-4,385,412.50	79
DOW 30		2001	816.00	5,736,865.50	79
Finance		2000	45.00	-507,100.70	79
Finance		2001	75.00	574,563.00	79
Media		2000	62.00	-465,393.90	79
Media		2001	58.00	386,853.60	79
Technology		2000	274.00	-1,116,767.25	79
Technology		2001	317.00	1,059,497.45	79

1. Format the Trans Year column and move it just to the right of the Portfolio Name column.

2. Insert a column to the right of Portfolio Name and insert another to the right of Revenue Expense.

3. Drag Num Calls from the Report Manager and drop it into the column to the right of Revenue Expense.

    Notice that it displays 79 for each cell in the column. This is the total number of calls made in the entire report. BusinessObjects does not know how to distribute the values, because the data providers are not linked.

4. Drag Call Port Mgr Phone from the Report Manager and try to drop it in the column to the right of Portfolio Name.

    You will not be able to drop it, because BusinessObjects does not know which number belongs to each portfolio. Even though you can look at it and and distribute the numbers properly, you have not instructed BusinessObjects, until you link the Data Providers.

- Data providers are linked by relating intersecting dimension objects that contain redundant information.
  - In our case, Portfolio Name to Call Portfolio Name, and Trans Year to Call Year.
  - The objects do not have to be named the same, but they must contain intersecting data. This relationship logically joins the rows in the two data providers.

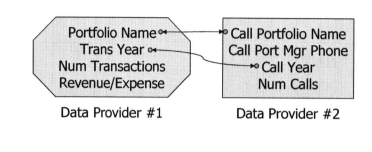

Data Provider #1   Data Provider #2

Since measures constantly re-aggregate and details are just attributes of dimensions, then dimensions must be the masters of each row of data in the data providers.

In the above case, Portfolio Name and Trans Year are the masters of Data Provider #1. This means that every row in the data set can be identified by the value of these dimensions. For example, DOW 30 – 2000, describes the row where all measures aggregate to these two values and all details support one of these two values.

In Data Provider #2, each unique row can be defined in a similar manner.

Now, if we link Portfolio Name to Call Portfolio Name, and Trans Year to Call Year, then the rows that have the same dimension values will join and make one virtual row that contains data from both data providers. If the relations are complete, every dimension in one set of data matches up to another in the other set, then the sets will combine to create one large set of data that is virtually as easy to work with as one large data provider.

- We link the dimensions in different data providers in the Data Manager.
- If the data providers were created from the same universe, then the dimensions with the same names will automatically link.

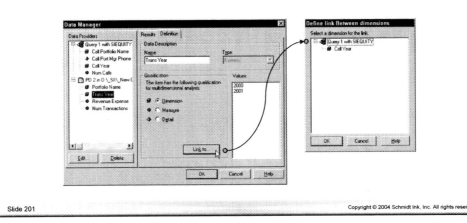

1. Select <u>Data->View Data...</u> from the menu.
2. Activate the Definition tab, by clicking on it.
3. Expand the first data provider in the list, by clicking on the plus sign preceding it.
4. Select the *Call Portfolio Name* object in the list.
5. Click the <u>Link to...</u> button.
6. Select *Portfolio Name* in the list of Dimensions.
7. Click the OK button.
8. Select the *Call Year* object in the list.
9. Click the <u>Link to...</u> button.
10. Select *Trans Year* in the list of Dimensions.
11. Click the OK button.

    Notice that there is a little arrow on the face of the dimension object in the data providers list. This means that the object is linked.

12. Click the OK button in the Data Manager.

    Notice that the Num Calls column now properly distributes the calls among the rows.

13. Drag the Call Port Mgr Phone detail from the Report Manager onto the column to the right of the Portfolio Name column.

- A document contains two data providers.
- A table contains objects from Data Provider A
  - A measure from Data Provider B can be inserted into the table.
    - If the Data Providers are not linked, then it will display the report total for the measure in every cell.
    - If the Data Providers are linked, it will display the proper value for each row.
    - If the data providers are partially linked, the it will display the value for the linked dimensions.

Portfolio Name	Trans Year	Num Calls
Alternative Energy	2000	79
Alternative Energy	2001	79
Biotech	2000	79
Biotech	2001	79
DOW 30	2000	79
DOW 30	2001	79
Finance	2000	79
Finance	2001	79
Media	2000	79
Media	2001	79
Technology	2000	79
Technology	2001	79

Unlinked

Portfolio Name	Trans Year	Num Calls
Alternative Energy	2000	
Alternative Energy	2001	
Biotech	2000	12
Biotech	2001	11
DOW 30	2000	18
DOW 30	2001	10
Finance	2000	8
Finance	2001	8
Media	2000	8
Media	2001	4
Technology	2000	
Technology	2001	

Linked

Portfolio Name	Trans Year	Num Calls
Alternative Energy	2000	
Alternative Energy	2001	
Biotech	2000	23
Biotech	2001	23
DOW 30	2000	28
DOW 30	2001	28
Finance	2000	16
Finance	2001	16
Media	2000	12
Media	2001	12
Technology	2000	
Technology	2001	

Linked on Portfolio

Measures always aggregate to the context in which they are placed. Contexts are defined by the dimensions in the context. If a measure from an unlinked data provider is placed in a context defined by dimensions in a different data provider, then the measure will simply aggregate to the report context, because there is no defined relationship between the measure's data provider and the context in which it is placed.

In the far-right table, the data providers are only linked on Portfolio Name and not on Trans Year. Therefore, the measure only realizes the relationship between it and Portfolio Name. Thus, it will only aggregate to the Portfolio and ignore the year component of the table.

A detail is supposed to have a special relationship with a dimension. It is only supposed to have one value per dimension value. For example, each employee id in a company can only have one name. Employee id would be the dimension and employee name would be the detail. If this is true, then it can do no harm to allow it to be inserted into a table, even though it has not been directly linked to a detail in the other data provider.

Unlinked dimensions cannot be allowed in a table that contains unlinked dimensions from another data provider, because it may cause the measures in the other data provider to aggregate multiple times (double-count). Therefore, BusinessObjects will not allow you to insert an unlinked dimension into a table that contains unlinked dimensions from another data provider.

One may argue that there is only one dimension value for each of the contexts defined by the linked dimensions in the table. This may happen when we include Product and Product ID. In these cases, you can force BusinessObjects to allow the insertion using the Max function, as shown above.

1. Select <u>Format->Filters...</u> from the menu.
2. Select the table to place the filter on in the <u>Filters On</u> list.
3. Click the Add... button.
4. Select *Portfolio Name* from the Variable(s) to Filter dialog.
5. Click the OK button to dismiss the Variable(s) to Filter dialog.
6. Click the Define... button in the Filters dialog.
7. Double-click the equals (=) operator in the <u>Operators</u> list.
8. Double-click Not in the <u>Operators</u> list.
9. Double-click IsNull in the Logical Functions folder.
10. Double-click the Num Calls object in the <u>Variables</u> list.

   You should now have the following formula:
   = Not IsNull(<Num Calls>)

11. Click the OK button.
12. Click the OK button in the Filters dialog.

   The filter now only shows rows of information for only the portfolios with non-NULL number of calls.

Erroneous Results from Multiple Data Providers

- Multiple data providers may cause erroneous results due to indirect linking.

- Suppose we have two data providers with the following:

Portfolio Name	Portfolio Mgr Name(Name)
Alternative Energy	David Balkcom
Biotech	Maria Castro
DOW 30	Sean Wilkenson
Finance	Robert Denning
Media	Kathy James
Technology	Eddie Wang

Portfolio Mgr Name(Num)	Num Transactions
David Balkcom	174
Eddie Wang	591
Kathy James	120
Maria Castro	184
Robert Denning	120
Sean Wilkenson	1,491

- Placing Portfolio Name and Num Transactions in a table will cause the following:

Portfolio Name	Num Transactions
Alternative Energy	2,680
Biotech	2,680
DOW 30	2,680
Finance	2,680
Media	2,680
Technology	2,680

- The MultiCube function will properly redistribute the measure values.

    =MultiCube(<Num Transactions>)

Portfolio Name	Num Transactions
Alternative Energy	174
Biotech	184
DOW 30	1,491
Finance	120
Media	120
Technology	591

1. Create a new document with the SI Equity universe. Select Portfolio Name and Portfolio Mgr Name.

2. Insert an additional data provider from SI Equity universe. Select Portfolio Mgr Name and Num Transactions.

    We do not have to link the data providers on the common dimension, as they will already be linked.

3. Create a new table using Portfolio Name and Num Transactions.

    Notice that the number of transactions is the same for each row. This seems awkward, because the relationship between Portfolio Name and Portfolio Mgr Name is one-to-one and it seems logical that the measures would report correctly.

4. Click on one of the Num Transaction values and modify the formula to =MultiCube(<Num Transactions>) and then press [Enter]

    The MultiCube function has rectified the values by instructing BusinessObjects that there is an indirect relationship between Portfolio Name and Num Transactions.

    When using this function, one must be positive that there is a one-to-one relationship between the dimensions. If this is not true the measures will redistribute incorrectly.

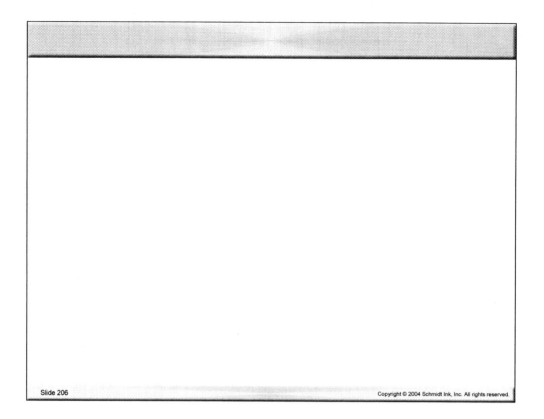

Advanced Course for BusinessObjects Reporter

Data and Report
Contexts

Introduction

- In this chapter, we are going to discuss report and data contexts within a document.
- We are going to explore different ways to manipulate these contexts to help us make more complex reports.
- We will cover context operators
  - In, ForAll, and ForEach
  - Where
- Most complex reports manipulate default contexts to achieve desired output from formulas

- Contexts in reports are created by structural breaks
  - Each row, header, break footer, section, and report header/footer are defined by different sets of dimension values
  - A sum in a row will aggregate for only that row; in a break footer, it will aggregate for all the rows in the break; in a report footer, it will aggregate for all of the rows in a report; and so forth

1. Create a report from the SI Equity universe

2. From the Portfolio class, select *Portfolio Name*, *Trans Year*, *Trans Quarter* and *Num Transactions*

3. Click Run

4. Set *Portfolio Name* as Master

   Click on any value in the column and then select Format->Set as Master from the menu.

5. Insert a break on *Trans Year*

   Select any value in the column and select Insert->Break from the menu

6. Place a sum on the *Num Transactions* column

   Click on any value in the column and select Data->Calculations->Sum from the menu.

   Notice that the sum is different in each of the contexts, even though the formula is the same for each context. The calculation engine in BusinessObjects sums the values based on the dimension values in the row.

   Details values also affect the calculations. However, since there is only suppose to be one detail value per dimension value, it usually does not affect the calculation.

209

- Dimension values also form contexts in data
    - Even though the data in not in a structure report, the dimension values can still form contexts within the data.
    - In the tables below, Portfolio Name and Tran Year form contexts.
    - Additional contexts can be form by combining the dimension values.
        - For example, Trans Year and Trans Quarter will form contexts:
            - 2000/3, 2000/4, 2001/1, 2001/2, 2001/3

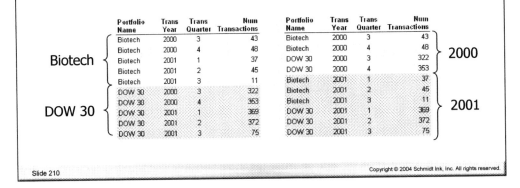

Knowledge of how the dimension values form contexts within the data will allow us to manipulate the data the form desired aggregates.

For example, in a normalization report, we want to divide every number in the report by some total in a report. A report normalized by year, will have every number in the report divided by the total for each number's respective year, as in the formula: x / (Sum(x) for the entire year).

Context Operators

- Context operators allow us to manipulate the data contexts and override the default report contexts.
- BusinessObjects supplies four different operators
    - In: The In operator allows us to choose which dimensions in a report context will affect our calculations.
    - ForAll: The ForAll operator allows us to instruct BusinessObjects which dimensions in a report context will not affect our calculations.
    - ForEach: The ForEach operator allows us to define groups within the data context for our calculations.
    - Where: The Where operator allows us to override existing contexts and aggregate to specific dimensions values.
- There is an example of each operator in the following slides.

The context operators allow us to override and redefine the default contexts in a report that are due to report structure. Master of these operators will allow the creation of more complex and compact reports, especially since most of the operators allow for summaries within contexts.

211

- The In operator allows us to choose which dimension(s) in a report define the context for an aggregate function.
  - In the example below, we chose the *Portfolio Name* dimension to define the context for our calculation.
    - Therefore, *Trans Year* and *Trans Quarter* no longer affect the calculation and it is only dependent on the values of the *Portfolio Name* object.
    - Therefore, in this example, the context in the Portfolio Total column is defined the same as the break footer.
  - The formula in the last column is a mixed context
    - = (<Num Transactions>) / (<Num Transactions> In <Portfolio Name>)
    - The numerator calculates within the default context defined by the report
    - The denominator calculates within the context defined by the In operator

Portfolio Name	Trans Year	Trans Quarter	Portfolio Total	Num Transactions	% Portfolio
DOW 30	2000	3	1,491	322	21.60 %
	2000	4	1,491	353	23.68 %
	2001	1	1,491	369	24.75 %
	2001	2	1,491	372	24.95 %
	2001	3	1,491	75	5.03 %
DOW 30			Sum:	1,491	100.00 %

1. Create a report from the SI Equity universe
2. From the Portfolio class, select *Portfolio Name*, *Trans Year*, *Trans Quarter* and *Num Transactions*
3. Click Run
4. Insert a break on *Portfolio Name*
5. Insert a sum on *Num Transactions*
6. Insert a column to the right of *Num Transactions*
7. Enter the following formula into the new column

   = <Num Transactions> In <Portfolio Name>

   Notice that the value in each row is the same as the value in the footer. The In operator has created a new context for each row that is defined only by the value of the *Portfolio Name* dimension.

8. Alter the new formula to the following

   = <Num Transactions> /
   <Num Transactions> In <Portfolio Name>

9. Format the cell to Percent Style.

212

- We use the In operator when we want to override existing contexts within a report
  - The default context for each row in this report is defined by Portfolio Name, Trans Year, and Trans Quarter
  - Each of the Report footer average calculations use a different context to define the sums before averaging
    - Row: Default
    - Portfolio: Portfolio Name
    - Yearly: Trans Year
    - Quarterly: Trans Quarter, Trans Year

Portfolio Name	Trans Year	Trans Quarter	Num Transactions
Biotech	2000	3	43
	2000	4	48
	2001	1	37
	2001	2	45
	2001	3	11
Biotech		Sum:	184
DOW 30	2000	3	322
	2000	4	353
	2001	1	369
	2001	2	372
	2001	3	75
DOW 30		Sum:	1,491
Finance	2000	3	24
	2000	4	21
	2001	1	34
	2001	2	32
	2001	3	9
Finance		Sum:	120
		Avg Row:	120
		Avg Portfolio:	598
		Avg Yearly:	398
		Avg Quarterly:	359

1. Create a report from the SI Equity universe
2. From the Portfolio class, select *Portfolio Name*, *Trans Year*, *Trans Quarter* and *Num Transactions*
3. Click Run
4. Insert a break on *Portfolio Name*
5. Insert a sum on *Num Transactions*
6. Insert three rows below the report footer row
7. Insert the following formulas into the rows

   = Average(<Num Transactions>)

   = Average(<Num Transactions> In <Portfolio Name>)

   = Average(<Num Transactions> In <Trans Year>)

   = Average(<Num Transactions> In (<Trans Quarter>, <Trans Year>))

   For the Avg Row, Avg Portfolio, Avg Yearly, and Avg Quarterly.

In Operator Context Definitions

- Any number of dimensions can define a context for the In operator. However, if there are more than one, they must be separated by commas, and enclosed in parentheses. This is also true for the ForAll and ForEach operators.
  - In (<Trans Year>, <Portfolio Name>)
- The In operator allows us to use keywords to define a context.
  - In Report: The entire report is the context
  - In Block: The entire section of a master-detail is the context
  - In Body: The current default context for the formula. Rarely needed, because it is redundant to the default report logic.
  - In CurrentPage: The page is the context
    Note: The CurrentPage context has been unreliable and should be used with caution. Please open the Context Keywords report for an example.

Context keywords allow us to place general contexts on the In operator. This helps ensure that, if a report is reformatted, then the formulas will have a higher probability of still being accurate.

In Block Example

- The In Block suffix allows us to override the default context of a table, xTab, or chart, and defines the context as the entire section of a Master-Detail report.
  - This keyword only works in sections of Master-Detail reports
  - The formula in the % Trans column is
    - = <Num Transactions> / <Num Transactions> In Block
  - As opposed to
    - = <Num Transactions> / <Num Transactions> In <Portfolio Name>
    - = <Num Transactions> / <Num Transactions> In <Portfolio Industry>

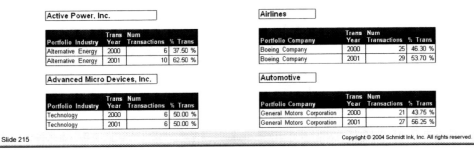

1. Create a report with *Portfolio Company*, *Portfolio Industry*, *Trans Year*, and *Num Transactions*

2. Click on any Portfolio Company and select <u>Format->Set as Master</u>

3. Insert a column to the right of Num Transactions and insert the following formula

   = <Num Transactions> / <Num Transactions> In Block

4. Format the cell as a percent

The column is now relatively safe from online analysis. Which means that someone can now drag the Portfolio Industry object and drop it on the Portfolio Company master cell. This will cause the Portfolio Industry to now become the master. The % Trans column will correctly conform to the new context.

If the % Trans column was hard coded to use the Portfolio Company, then when Portfolio Industry became the master, the % Trans column would of become confusing and ambiguous.

215

Report Normalization with the In Operator

- **The In operator enables us to view percent distribution across dimensions or a report**
    - The middle table shows the percent distribution across the years in a report.
    - The table, on the right, shows the percent distribution across the entire report.

	2000	2001	Sum:
Alternative Energy	78	96	174
Biotech	91	93	184
DOW 30	675	816	1,491
Finance	45	75	120
Media	62	58	120
Technology	274	317	591
Sum:	1,225	1,455	2,680

	2000	2001
Alternative Energy	6 %	7 %
Biotech	7 %	6 %
DOW 30	55 %	56 %
Finance	4 %	5 %
Media	5 %	4 %
Technology	22 %	22 %
Sum:	100 %	100 %

Normal to Trans Year

	2000	2001	Sum:
Alternative Energy	3 %	4 %	6 %
Biotech	3 %	3 %	7 %
DOW 30	25 %	30 %	56 %
Finance	2 %	3 %	4 %
Media	2 %	2 %	4 %
Technology	10 %	12 %	22 %
Sum:	46 %	54 %	100 %

Normal to Report

1. Create a report from the SI Equity universe

2. From the Portfolio class, select *Portfolio Name*, *Trans Year*, and *Num Transactions*

3. Click Run

4. Format the table into an xtab with the Trans Year across the top

5. Click on any number in the xtab and then select Data->Calculations->Sum from the menu.

6. Copy the table and modify the measure formula to

    = <Num Transactions>/<Num Transactions> In <Trans Year>

    This will normalize Num Transactions to Trans Year.

7. Format the measure cells to percent

8. Copy the measure formula to the total cells in the xtab

    The total of each column should be 1 or 100%

9. The row totals and report total really do not make too much sense and they are usually deleted.

10. Copy the original xtab and modify the measure formula to

    = <Num Transactions>/<Num Transactions> In Report

    This will normalize Num Transactions to the report

11. Format the measure cells to percent

12. Copy the measure formula to the total cells in the xtab

    The column totals should be the percentage of transactions in each year

    The row totals are the percentage of transactions in each portfolio

    The report total should be 1 or 100%

216

The ForAll Operator

- The ForAll operator allows us to choose which dimension(s) in a report will not be part of the definition of a context for an aggregate function.
  - In the example below, we chose to ignore *Trans Year* and *Trans Quarter*, thus the remaining dimension, *Portfolio Name,* defines the context for the calculation.
    - Therefore, *Trans Year* and *Trans Quarter* no longer affect the calculation and it is only dependent on the values of the *Portfolio Name* object.
  - The formula in the last column is a mixed context
    - = <Num Transactions> / <Num Transactions> ForAll (<Trans Year>, <Trans Quarter>)
    - The numerator calculates within the default context defined by the report
    - The denominator calculates within the context defined by the ForAll operator

Portfolio Name	Trans Year	Trans Quarter	Portfolio Total	Num Transactions	% Portfolio
DOW 30	2000	3	1,491	322	21.60 %
	2000	4	1,491	353	23.68 %
	2001	1	1,491	369	24.75 %
	2001	2	1,491	372	24.95 %
	2001	3	1,491	75	5.03 %
DOW 30			Sum:	1,491	100.00 %

1. Create a report from the SI Equity universe
2. From the Portfolio class, select *Portfolio Name*, *Trans Year*, *Trans Quarter* and *Num Transactions*
3. Click Run
4. Insert a break on *Portfolio Name*
5. Insert a sum on *Num Transactions*
6. Insert a column to the right of *Num Transactions*
7. Enter the following formula into the new column

   =<Num Transactions> ForAll (<Trans Year> , <Trans Quarter>)
   Notice that the value in each row is the same as the value in the footer. The ForEach operator has created a new context for each row that is defined only by the value of the *Portfolio Name* dimension, by ignoring the Trans Year and Trans Quarter values.

8. Alter the new formula to the following

   = <Num Transactions> / <Num Transactions> ForAll (<Trans Year> , <Trans Quarter>)

9. Format the cell to Percent Style.

217

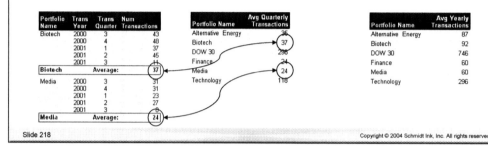
1. Create a report from the SI Equity universe

2. From the Portfolio class, select *Portfolio Name*, *Trans Year*, *Trans Quarter* and *Num Transactions*

3. Click Run

4. Delete the *Trans Year* and *Trans Quarter* columns

5. Alter the formula in the *Num Transactions* column to

    =Average(<Num Transactions> ForEach (<Trans Year> , <Trans Quarter>))

6. Change the *Num Transactions* column header to

    Avg Quarterly Transactions

7. Insert a column to the right of the *Avg Quarterly Transactions* column

8. Enter the following formula

    = Average(<Num Transactions> ForEach (<Trans Year>))

9. Enter the header

    Avg Yearly Transactions

    Do you think that the following formula,
    = *Average(<Num Transactions> ForEach (<Trans Quarter>))*,
    would give desired results? Probably not. This would not give the average of the prior 5 quarters. It would yield the average of the total for each of the four quarter numbers.

218

ForEach Operator Defines Report Contexts

- The ForEach operator will add additional dimensions to the context definition
  - In the top report, the default context is Portfolio Name, Trans Year, and Trans Quarter
  - The average in each footer averages the Number of Transactions in each row of the footer, which is defined by the default context
  - Since the bottom table's default context is defined only by Portfolio Name, the average for each portfolio is simply its sum
    - Average (*Sum*(Num Transactions))
  - The ForEach operator allowed us to add dimensions to the existing default context.
    - ForEach (*Portfolio Name*, Trans Year, Trans Quarter)

Portfolio Name	Trans Year	Trans Quarter	Num Transactions
Biotech	2000	3	43
	2000	4	48
	2001	1	37
	2001	2	45
	2001	3	
Biotech			37
DOW 30	2000	3	322
	2000	4	353
	2001	1	369
	2001	2	372
	2001	3	
DOW 30			298
Finance	2000	3	24
	2000	4	21
	2001	1	34
	2001	2	32
	2001	3	
Finance			24
		Average:	120

Portfolio Name	Average Num Transactions
Biotech	37
DOW 30	298
Finance	24

1. Create a report from the SI Equity universe

2. From the Portfolio class, select *Portfolio Name*, *Trans Year*, *Trans Quarter* and *Num Transactions*

3. Click Run

4. Delete the *Trans Year* and *Trans Quarter* columns

5. Alter the formula in the *Num Transactions* column to

   =Average(<Num Transactions> ForEach (<Trans Year> , <Trans Quarter>))

6. Change the *Num Transactions* column header to

   Average Num Transactions

219

- Year - Quarter resolution
    - = Average(<Num Transactions> ForEach
    (<Trans Year>, <Trans Quarter>))

Portfolio Name	Trans Year	Trans Quarter	Num Transactions
Biotech	2000	3	43
Biotech	2000	4	48
Biotech	2001	1	37
Biotech	2001	2	45
Biotech	2001	3	11

Portfolio Name	Num Transactions
Biotech	37
DOW 30	298
Finance	24

$(43+48+37+45+11)/5 = 37$

- Year Resolution
    - = Average(<Num Transactions> ForEach (<Trans Year>))

Portfolio Name	Trans Year	Trans Quarter	Num Transactions
Biotech	2000	3	43
Biotech	2000	4	48
Biotech	2001	1	37
Biotech	2001	2	45
Biotech	2001	3	11

Portfolio Name	Num Transactions
Biotech	92
DOW 30	746
Finance	60

$(91+93)/2 = 92$

Do you think that the following formula,
= Average(<Num Transactions> ForEach (<Trans Quarter>)), would give desired results? Probably not. This would not give the average of the prior 5 quarters. It would yield the average of the total for each of the four quarter numbers.

Combining Context Operators

- **Combining Context operators allows more complex formulas**
  - For example, to calculate the variance from the portfolio mean, we could use the following formula
    - = <Num Transactions> - Average(<Num Transactions> ForEach (<Trans Quarter>,<Trans Year>)) In <Portfolio Name>
    - The ForEach operator instructs the Average function to average the totals for each Trans Quarter – Trans Year combination.
    - The In operator instructs the average function to average the combinations within each portfolio.
  - To calculate the variance from the report mean, we could use the following formula
    - = <Num Transactions> - Average(<Num Transactions> ForEach (<Trans Quarter> ,<Trans Year>)) In Report

Portfolio Name	Trans Year	Trans Quarter	Num Transactions	Variance from Portfolio Mean	Variance form Report Mean
Alternative Energy	2000	3	42	7	-47
Alternative Energy	2000	4	36	1	-53
Alternative Energy	2001	1	49	14	-40
Alternative Energy	2001	2	36	1	-53
Alternative Energy	2001	3	11	-24	-78

Portfolio Mean: 35
Report Mean: 89

People often talk about input and output contexts, which is probably confusing to most. It is probably better to think what the context operators are doing in the formula. For example, in this case, we want to calculate the average quarterly number of transactions, so we use Average(<Num Transactions) For Each (Trans Quarter>, <Trans Year>). The next question is, do we want this average for every portfolio or for the entire report. Thus, we can use In <Portfolio Name> or In Report, respectively.

1. Create a report with *Portfolio Name, Trans Year, Trans Quarter* and *Num Transactions*
2. Click Run
3. Insert two columns to the right of Num Transactions.
4. In the first new column insert the formula
   = <Num Transactions> - Average(<Num Transactions> For Each (<Trans Year>, <Trans Quarter>)) In <Portfolio Name>
5. In the second new column enter the formula
   = <Num Transactions> - Average(<Num Transactions> For Each (<Trans Year>, <Trans Quarter>)) In Report

In this example, the In operator allows us to override the existing natural contexts in the report. A natural context is defined by the dimensions in the report. In this case – Portfolio Name, Trans Year, and Trans Quarter. In In operator allows us to calculate for the portfolio context and the report context. The For Each operator allows us to average for the Year – quarter combinations within these two contexts.

221

The Where Operator

- The Where operator allows us to isolate measures to selected dimension values within a report context.
    - For example, the following formula will override any context in a report created by Portfolio Name. Thus causing Num Transactions to only aggregate for the portfolio DOW 30.
      = <Num Transactions>
          Where (<Portfolio Name>="DOW 30")

Portfolio Name	Total Transactions	DOW30 Transactions
Alternative Energy	174	1,491
Biotech	184	1,491
DOW 30	1,491	1,491
Finance	120	1,491
Media	120	1,491
Technology	591	1,491

    - The Where clause will not override other report contexts defined by other dimensions.
        - In the table to the right, the Trans Year dimension has divided the DOW 30 number of transactions.

Portfolio Name	Trans Year	Total Transactions	DOW30 Transactions	% of DOW30 Transactions
Alternative Energy	2000	78	675	12 %
Alternative Energy	2001	96	816	12 %
Biotech	2000	91	675	13 %
Biotech	2001	93	816	11 %
DOW 30	2000	675	675	100 %
DOW 30	2001	816	816	100 %
Finance	2000	45	675	7 %
Finance	2001	75	816	9 %
Media	2000	62	675	9 %
Media	2001	58	816	7 %
Technology	2000	274	675	41 %
Technology	2001	317	816	39 %

1. Create a report from the SI Equity universe

2. From the Portfolio class, select *Portfolio Name*, *Trans Year*, and *Num Transactions*

3. Click Run

4. Insert two columns to the right of Num Transactions

5. Rename the Num Transactions header to Total Transactions

6. Insert the following formula into the next column

    = <Num Transactions> Where (<Portfolio Name> = "DOW 30")

7. Insert the following into the header

    DOW30 Transactions

8. Insert the following formula into the remaining column

    =<Num Transactions> /
        <Num Transactions> Where (<Portfolio Name>="DOW 30")

9. Insert the following into the header

    % of DOW30 Transactions

    Notice that the Where clause only applies to the denominator and the the numerator is still operating under normal context rules.

Rest of World Example

- The Where operator allows us to isolate selected dimension values. However, when used in a formula, it can also allow us to isolate the rest of the world.

  - = <Num Transactions>
      Where (<Portfolio Name>="DOW 30")
    allowed us to to isolate the number of DOW 30 transactions

  - = <Num Transactions> -
      <Num Transactions> Where (<Portfolio Name>="DOW 30")
    this formula will subtract the DOW 30 transactions from the total transactions, thus the rest of the world.

Trans Year	Trans Quarter	Total Transactions	DOW30 Transactions	Rest of Transactions	% DOW30 Transactions
2000	3	588	322	266	55 %
2000	4	637	353	284	55 %
2001	1	645	369	276	57 %
2001	2	643	372	271	58 %
2001	3	167	75	92	45 %

1. Create a report from the SI Equity universe

2. From the Portfolio class, select *Portfolio Name*, *Trans Year*, *Trans Quarter* and *Num Transactions*

3. Click Run

4. Insert three columns to the right of Num Transactions

5. Delete the Portfolio Name column

6. Change the Num Transactions header to Total Transactions

7. Enter the following formula into the next column

    = <Num Transactions> Where (<Portfolio Name>="DOW 30")

8. Change the header to

    DOW 30 Transactions

9. Enter the following formula into the next column

    = <Num Transactions> -
        <Num Transactions> Where (<Portfolio Name>="DOW 30")

10. Change the header to

    Rest of Transactions

11. Enter the following formula into the remaining column

    =(<Num Transactions> Where (<Portfolio Name>="DOW 30")) /
        <Num Transactions>

12. Change the header to

    % DOW 30 Transactions

223

Where Operator Restrictions

- The Where operator only allows the following
  - Equals operator:
    =<Num Transactions> Where (<Trans Year>=2000)
    - It does not allow: <>, <=, >=, <, >, InList, Between, …
  - And logic
    =<Num Transactions>
    Where (<Trans Year>=2000 And <Trans Quarter> = 1)
    - It does not allow Or's
- We can use more complicated logic, if we encapsulate it within a variable that uses If-Then logic.
  - For example, a variable named *First Half* may have the following formula: = If <Trans Quarter> InList (1, 2) Then 1 Else 0
  - Then the Where clause would be
    = <Num Transactions> Where (<First Half> = 1)

We will cover If-then logic later in this course. Until then, we will use simplistic versions of it to further enhance our Where operator study.

Many people get frustrated, because of the logic limitations on the Where operator. However, as shown above these limitations are easily overcome with the use of the If-Then-Else statement. Most report developers that I know, now always use the If-Then-Else logic, even for simple logic, such as <Trans Year> = 2000.

Prompted Rest of World Example

- In this example, we are going to modify the previous Rest of World example to use prompted input to select the portfolio of interest.
- Since the Where operator will not work with functions, we will use If-Then logic encapsulated in a variable. The variable will have the following
    - Name: IsPortfolioName
    - Formula:
      = If UserResponse (DataProvider(<Portfolio Name>) ,
        "Enter Portfolio:") = <Portfolio Name> Then 1 Else 0

Trans Year	Trans Quarter	Total Transactions	DOW30 Transactions	Rest of Transactions	% DOW30 Transactions
2000	3	588	322	266	55 %
2000	4	637	353	284	55 %
2001	1	645	369	276	57 %
2001	2	643	372	271	58 %
2001	3	167	75	92	45 %

1. Modify the query of the previous report to contain the following condition

   Portfolio Name Less than Prompt ('Enter Portfolio')

   Or

   Portfolio Name Greater than or equal to Prompt ('Enter Portfolio')

2. Click Run and select any portfolio

3. Create the following variable

   Name: IsPortfolioName

   Formula: = If UserResponse(DataProvider(<Portfolio Name>),
   "Enter Portfolio:") = <Portfolio Name> Then 1 Else 0

4. Change the DOW 30 Transactions header to

   = UserResponse(DataProvider(<Portfolio Name>) ,"Enter Portfolio:") + "
   Transactions"

5. Enter the following Formula

   = <Num Transactions> Where (<IsPortfolioName> = 1)

6. In the Rest of Transactions column, enter the following formula

   = <Num Transactions> -
   <Num Transactions> Where (<IsPortfolioName> = 1)

7. Change the column header in the last column to

   = "% " + UserResponse(DataProvider(<Portfolio Name>) ,
   "Enter Portfolio:") + " Transactions"

8. Enter the following formula into the column

   =(<Num Transactions> Where (<IsPortfolioName> = 1)) /
   <Num Transactions>

225

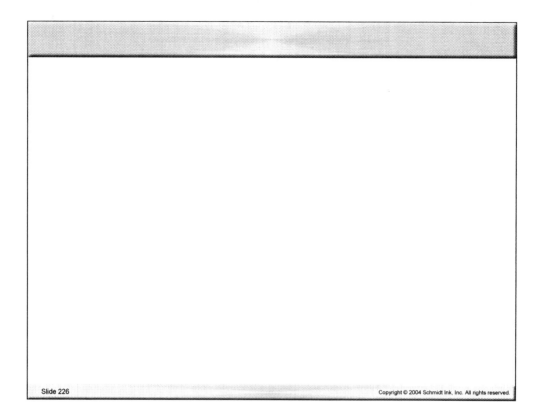

Advanced Course for BusinessObjects Reporter

Formulas, Variables
And
Various Functions

Introduction

- In this chapter, we will cover formulas and variables, and how to use them to create desired results in our documents.
    - We will learn about formula syntax
    - We will learn how to create a variable
    - We are going to look at each of the function groups and create sample reports with functions from many of the groups
    - We will look at the If-Then-Else logic structure

Formula Syntax

- A formula in BusinessObjects is any expression that begins with an equal sign (=).
    - = Hi, = 5, = <Num Transactions> + 5, = "Hi"
    - All of the above is a valid formula, except the first (= Hi).
- Syntax is a formula's structure
    - All formulas must begin with an equal sign (=)
    - All text must be enclosed in double quotes
    - All objects and variables must be enclosed in angle-brackets.
        - = <Num Transactions>
    - The condition in a Where operator must be in parentheses
        - = <Num Transactions> Where (<Trans Year> = 2000)
    - If there is more than one object in a context operator list, then they must be separated by commas and be enclosed in parentheses
        - = <Num Transactions> In (<Trans Year>, <Portfolio Name>)

Formula syntax is important, because BusinessObjects will not accept a formula, unless is has proper syntax. The rules are simple and the Help file often has examples of proper syntax for the functions.

Some formulas are very complicated and it is hard for most people to understand the syntax. However, most formulas that are needed in reports are not that complex and with a little practice, the proper syntax can be easily achieved.

Formula syntax also follows the basic order of operations learned for math. Do what is inside the parentheses first, then multiply, then divide, then add, then subtract.

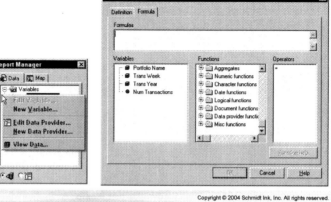

Variables are sometimes easier to use than formulas, because they are less bulky and can be represented like any other object in the data provider.

In this example, we are simply going to encapsulate a measure within a variable. This is often very useful, because after complicated reports are created, it is not uncommon to change the measure in the report. This usually means changing every formula in the report to accept the new measure. Not only is this a slow and frustrating process, it can also be very prone to errors.

1. Create a document with Portfolio Name, Trans Year, and Revenue/Expense

2. Select the data in the Revenue/Expense column by clicking on any of the values

3. Select Data->Variables… from the menu

4. Click the Add… button

5. On the Definition tab, in the Name Field enter

    Revenue

6. On the Formula tab, in the Formulas field enter

    = <Revenue/Expense>

7. Click OK, click Replace

230

Functions

- Functions return information or results to a formula
  - = Sum (<x>), = CurrentDate(), = ToNumber("5"), ...
  - Functions can return a date, text, or a number.
- Functions can accept arguments
  - An argument is the data within the parentheses that supply information to the function.
  - Arguments can be dates, text, numbers, or functions
- The proper syntax for each function is displayed in the Formula Editor.
  - Notice the display in the lower-left of the editor that displays the proper syntax for the Count function.

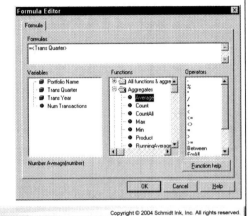

Functions are supplied by BusinessObjects to make the program more powerful. Functions allow us to operate on text, dates, and numbers. They are often used to Sum, Count, Min, Max, and so forth.

Functions allow us to manipulate data in reports. For example, suppose that the dates returned to our report were formatted as text. However, we want to sort our report in chronological order. If we sort the text dates, they will sort in alphabetical order and this is usually not what we want. To convert the text dates to dates, we use the ToDate function

= ToDate(<TextDate>, "MM/DD/YYYY").

There are many functions supplied with BusinessObjects and many of them are used by experience report writers everyday.

- Aggregate functions operate on all of an object's values in a context.
  - For example, sum(<Num Transactions>) will sum the number of transactions in a column, in a break, in a section, ...
- Aggregate functions normally accept only numbers for arguments.
  - Count, Min, and Max are exceptions.
  - We often use the Min or Max function to rectify a #MULTIVALUE error

Portfolio Name	Trans Year	Num Transactions	Num Transactions
Alternative Energy	2000	78	= Sum(<Num Transactions>)
	2001	96	= Sum(<Num Transactions>)
Alternative Energy	Sum:	174	= Sum(<Num Transactions>)
Biotech	2000	91	= Sum(<Num Transactions>)
	2001	93	= Sum(<Num Transactions>)
Biotech	Sum:	184	= Sum(<Num Transactions>)
DOW 30	2000	675	= Sum(<Num Transactions>)
	2001	816	= Sum(<Num Transactions>)
DOW 30	Sum:	1,491	= Sum(<Num Transactions>)
Finance	2000	45	= Sum(<Num Transactions>)
	2001	75	= Sum(<Num Transactions>)
Finance	Sum:	120	= Sum(<Num Transactions>)
Media	2000	62	= Sum(<Num Transactions>)
	2001	58	= Sum(<Num Transactions>)
Media	Sum:	120	= Sum(<Num Transactions>)
Technology	2000	274	= Sum(<Num Transactions>)
	2001	317	= Sum(<Num Transactions>)
Technology	Sum:	591	= Sum(<Num Transactions>)
	Sum:	2,680	= Sum(<Num Transactions>)

Aggregate functions operate on sets of data. They sum, count, min, max, average, and find the variance.

The #MULTIVALUE occurs when a dimension is placed in a single cell, such as a header or footer cell, or a freestanding cell. This happens, because most dimensions have more than one value and, even if it only has one value, there is no guarantee that there won't be more in the future.

Since aggregate functions operate on sets of data, then it is reasonable to think that the max function will return the dimension value with the highest alpha value. However, if there is only one value for the dimension, then it will simply return that value. Hence, if there is only one dimension value per context in a report, then the formula

    = Max(<Dimension>),

will allow the insertion of a dimension into a single cell.

- Measures often have built-in aggregate functions.

Portfolio Name	Trans Year	Num Transactions	Num Transactions
Alternative Energy	2000	78	= <Num Transactions>
	2001	96	= <Num Transactions>
Alternative Energy	Sum:	174	= <Num Transactions>

  - Most often, it is the Sum function
  - The Universe designer assigns the aggregate to the measure when it is created.
- The built-in function will always execute before any applied functions.
  - For example, with the formula
    = Average(<Num Transactions>),
    the number of transactions will conform to
    the report context, before they are averaged.

Portfolio Name	Trans Year	Num Transactions
Alternative Energy	2000	78
Alternative Energy	2001	96
Biotech	2000	91
Biotech	2001	93
DOW 30	2000	675
DOW 30	2001	816
Finance	2000	45
Finance	2001	75
Media	2000	62
Media	2001	58
Technology	2000	274
Technology	2001	317
	Average:	223

Portfolio Name	Num Transactions
Alternative Energy	174
Biotech	184
DOW 30	1,491
Finance	120
Media	120
Technology	591
Average:	447

Average:	2,680

Most measures have built-in aggregate functions that define how the measure will conform to different contexts within a report. As can be seen from the slide, the measures will conform to a context, before any external aggregate function is applied to the measure. This causes a weird anomaly, the average of a report can also be the sum.

To rectify this anomaly, BusinessObjects supplies with context operators that will override the default report context for a measure. In this example, the ForEach operator will allow us to properly represent the averages in a freestanding cell.

1. Create a document with Portfolio Name, Trans Year, and Num Transactions.

2. Create the tables shown in the slide.

3. To show the average number of transactions for each year and portfolio, use the following formula

   = Average(<Num Transactions> ForEach
   (<Portfolio Name> , <Trans Year>))

Average:	223

4. To show the average number of transactions for each portfolio, use the following formula

   = Average(<Num Transactions> ForEach <Portfolio Name>)

Average:	447

233

- Dimensions differ from measures and details, because they
  - have no built-in aggregate functions
  - usually do not have a one-to-one relationship with other dimensions
  - usually have more than one value in a document
- These differences prevent dimensions from
  - being placed in a freestanding cell, such as a title, because they cannot conform to a smaller context.
    - Which dimension value should be displayed
  - being placed in a column of a table, where that table contains dimensions that are unlinked to the dimension.
    - Multiple dimension values will cause measures to double-count.
- If there is only one value for the dimension, or if the dimension shares a one-to-one relationship with unlinked dimensions, then we can use an aggregate to insert the dimension into a freestanding cell or table.

1. Create a document with *Portfolio Name*, *Trans Year*, and *Revenue/Expense*. Place the following condition *Trans Year* Equal to 2000. Then click Run

2. Insert a new query with *Portfolio Name* and *Portfolio Mgr Name*. Click Run.

3. Insert a column in the table after Portfolio Name and try to drop Portfolio Mgr Name into the new column.

   > It will not allow you to insert it, because it is an unlinked dimension. However, you realize that there is only one Mgr Name per portfolio and therefore, should be allowed to insert the dimension.

4. Enter the following formula into the new column

   = Max(<Portfolio Mgr Name>)

   This will rectify the conflict.

5. Drag the Trans Year object from the table to the Report Title cell. Just before you drop it, hold down the [Ctrl] to copy it.

   > This will cause the Report Title cell to display the #MULTIVALUE error. It is a multivalue error, because BusinessObjects assumes that dimension have more than one value. We know that there is only one Trans Year value, but BusinessObjects does not.

6. Change the formula in the Report Title cell to

   = Max(<Trans Year>)

- Running aggregates incrementally aggregate columns of data. They allow you to see an aggregate total as it evolves
- This table has two running sums in the last columns
    - Acc Comp sums the number of calls made by the entire company, thus it keeps summing through the break
    - Acc Man sum sums only for each manager, thus it resets with each new manager
- The Acc Man column uses a reset argument to reset the aggregate with each new manager.
- The two basic formulas are the following
    - = RunningSum(<Num Calls>)
    - = RunningSum(<Num Calls>; <Call Port Mgr Name>)

Call Port Mgr Name	Call Quarter	Num Calls	Acc Man	% Man Calls	% Comp Calls	Acc Comp	% Total Calls
Kathy James	1	1	1	8 %	3 %	1	3 %
	2	2	3	25 %	9 %	3	9 %
	3	5	8	67 %	23 %	8	23 %
	4	4	12	100 %	34 %	12	34 %
Kathy James		12	12	100 %	34 %	12	34 %
Maria Castro	1	8	8	35 %	23 %	20	57 %
	2	3	11	48 %	31 %	23	66 %
	3	10	21	91 %	60 %	33	94 %
	4	2	23	100 %	66 %	35	100 %
Maria Castro		23	23	100 %	66 %	35	100 %
Total:		35				35	100 %

1. Create a document with *Call Port Mgr Name*, *Call Quarter*, and *Num Calls*

2. Insert five columns to the right of the Num Calls column

3. Insert a break on *Call Port Mgr Name*

4. Enter the following formula into Acc Man

    = RunningSum(<Num Calls>; <Call Port Mgr Name>)

5. Enter the following formula into % Man Calls

    = RunningSum(<Num Calls>; <Call Port Mgr Name>) / <Num Calls> In <Call Port Mgr Name>

6. Enter the following formula into % Comp Calls

    = RunningSum(<Num Calls>; <Call Port Mgr Name>) / <Num Calls> In Report

7. Enter the following formula into Acc Comp

    = RunningSum(<Num Calls>)

8. Enter the following formula into % Total Calls

    = RunningSum(<Num Calls>) / <Num Calls> In Report

To make the table look exactly like the one in the slide, you can insert a column to the right of % Comp Calls and format it with no shading and no borders.

- Numeric functions operate only on the current number in a context. They do not aggregate, as the aggregate functions.
- Numeric functions consist of rounding and mathematical functions, with a few exceptions
  - Rank, this function accepts two arguments – a dimension and a measure. It then ranks the dimension based on the aggregation of the measure.
    - Rank(<Portfolio Name>, <Revenue/Expense>)
  - ToNumber, this function converts a text representation of a number to a numeric number.
    - This is often used in If-then statements when comparing text numbers to numeric numbers.
      - If ToNumber(<TextNumber>) = 5 Then …

- While the Numeric function may seem simple, they can allow us to create very efficient reports.
    - For example, the following report using the ToNumber function to allow us to create a Whole Year – Month to Date Revenue report (With a signal query).

Portfolio Name	Portfolio Company	WY 2000 Revenue	MTD 2001 Revenue
Alternative Energy	Active Power, Inc.	-17,559	26,381
	AstroPower, Inc.	2,809	11,275
	Ballard Power Systems Inc	-16,380	-22,478
	Capstone Turbine Corporation	7,636	27,607
	Electric Fuel Corporation	-9,571	4,803
	FuelCell Energy, Inc	9,343	-61,581
	H Power Corp	-24,469	-7,484
	Plug Power Inc.	-41,019	35,828
Alternative Energy		-89,221	14,341

1. Create a report with Portfolio Name, Portfolio Company, Trans Year, Trans Month, and Revenue/ Expense. Use the following condition
    - Drag Trans Month to the Conditions window
    - Double-click Less Than Or Equal To
    - Double-click Type a New Prompt, and enter - Enter Current Month Number:
    - Drag Trans Month to the Conditions window
    - Double-click Greater Than
    - Double-click Show List of Prompts and select - Enter Current Month Number:
2. Change the And operator to an Or operator, if necessary
3. Click Run
4. Enter 3 in the prompt dialog
5. Delete the Trans Year, Trans Month, and Revenue/ Expense columns.
6. Create the following two variables
    - Name: CurrentMonth
    - Formula: =ToNumber(UserResponse(DataProvider(<Portfolio Company>) ,"Enter Current Month Number:"))
    - Name: IsMTD2001
    - Formula: = If <Trans Year>=2001 And <Trans Month> <= <CurrentMonth> Then 1 Else 0
7. Insert two columns with the following formulas
    - Header: WY 2000 Revenue
    - =<Revenue/ Expense> Where (<Trans Year>=2000)
    - Header: MTD 2001 Revenue
    - =<Revenue/ Expense> Where (<IsMTD2001>=1)

- The Rank function allows us to rank dimensions in our reports by some measure in the report.
  - In this example, we will rank the top company in each portfolio, We will then echo the top company in the footer and compare it to the total companies within each portfolio.

Portfolio Name	Portfolio Company	Company Rank	Revenue/ Expense
Alternative Energy	Active Power, Inc.	4	19,648
	AstroPower, Inc.	7	3,620
	Ballard Power Systems Inc	5	14,998
	Capstone Turbine Corporation	2	52,855
	Electric Fuel Corporation	8	-2,507
	FuelCell Energy, Inc.	1	90,575
	H Power Corp.	6	7,436
	Plug Power Inc.	3	28,036
Total Companies			214,665
#1 Company	FuelCell Energy, Inc.		90,575
Rest of Companies			124,090
% #1 Company			42 %

1. Create a report with Portfolio Name, Portfolio Company, and Revenue/ Expense
2. Click Run
3. Place a break on Portfolio Name
4. Click on any Revenue/Expense value and click the Insert Sum button
5. Click on the footer row and insert three rows below the current footer
6. Insert a column to the left of Revenue/Expense
7. Insert the following into the new column
   - Header: Company Rank
   - Formula: = Rank(<Portfolio Company> ,<Revenue/ Expense>)
8. Create the following variable
   - Name: CompanyRank
     Formula: = Rank(<Portfolio Company> ,<Revenue/ Expense>)
   - Qualification: Measure
9. In the second footer row enter the following
   - #1 Company
   - = Max(If <CompanyRank>= 1 Then <Portfolio Company>)
   - = Max(If <CompanyRank>= 1 Then <Revenue/ Expense>)
10. In the third footer row enter the following
    - Rest of Companies
    - =<Revenue/ Expense> -
      Max(If <CompanyRank>= 1 Then <Revenue/ Expense>)
11. In the forth row enter the following
    - % #1 Company
    - = Max(If <CompanyRank>= 1 Then <Revenue/ Expense>) /
      <Revenue/ Expense>

238

- Character functions allow us to manipulate text in our reports. Many of these functions are used often, below are a few examples
  - To insert a return character into text
    - "First Line" + char(13) + "Second Line"
  - To remove return characters
    - Replace(<Text>, char(13), " ")
  - To concatenate a date to text
    - <Text> + " " + FormatDate(<Date>, "Mmm dd YYYY")
  - To concatenate a number to text
    - <Text> + " " + FormatNumber(<Number>, "00000")
  - To isolate first name
    - SubStr(<Portfolio Mgr Name> ,1 , Pos(<Portfolio Mgr Name>, " ") -1)
- The examples are almost endless and increase as the skill of the use of these functions increase.

- The Format functions, FormatDate and FormatNumber, convert dates and numbers to text.
  - Formatted data will only sort and behave like text
    - 01/01/2003
    - 01/01/2004
    - 01/02/2003
    - 01/02/2004
- If the data is to behave as it's native type, then it is better to use the Format->Cell dialog
  - Since characters represent the formats in the Format Cell dialog, a backslash must precede formatting characters to make them literals
    - Tra\de \Date: Mm/dd/yy
    - Num Transactions: 0

1. Create a document with *Portfolio Mgr Name*, *Trans Date*, and *Num Transactions*

2. Insert a column to the right of Trans Date and copy the Trans Date formula into the column.

3. Modify the first Trans Date column to the following formula

    = "Trade Date: " + FormatDate(<Trans Date> , "mm/dd/yy")

4. Select the second Trans Date column

5. Select Format->Cell... from the menu

6. Click the Number Tab to activate it

7. Select the Date/Time category

8. Enter the following into the Data/Time format field

    Tra\de \Date: mm/dd/yy

9. Resort the table by placing a sort on the newly formatted column

The column with the FormatDate function will sort as text and not in chronological order. However, the formatted date column will still sort in chronological order, because the contents are still a date.

The backslashes are needed, because the 'd' character extracts the day number of the date. Without the backslashes the field may display

    Tra5e 5ate: 01/05/2004

- Date functions allow us to manipulate dates in a document. Many of these functions are often used.
  - To display the day name of a date
    - DayName(<date>)
  - To extract the day number of a month
    - DayNumberOfMonth(<date>)
  - The extract the number of days between two dates
    - DaysBetween(<date1>, <date2>)
  - To display the last day of the month for a date
    - LastDayOfMonth(<date>)
  - To display the number of months between two dates
    - MonthsBetween(<date>)
  - To convert a text date to a date
    - ToDate(<Text Date>, "Mm/dd/yyyy")
    - "Mm/dd/yyyy" represents the format of the text date and may vary

- In this example, we will create a month end report. We will use many of the skills that we have learned in this chapter.
- The report shows the monthly revenue for each portfolio. It also displays the running sum of the revenue for each portfolio. The revenue is displayed in thousandths.

	Jul 00	Aug 00	Sep 00	Oct 00	Nov 00	Dec 00	Jan 01	Feb 01	Mar 01	Apr 01	May 01	Jun 01	Jul 01	Sum:
Alternative Energy	-132	-72	205	25	-103	-11	37	40	-63	4	149	75	62	215
Alternative Energy	-132	-204	1	25	-78	-89	-53	-12	-75	-71	78	153	215	
Biotech	-22	-302	-78	67	-14	-22	-28	19	-111	107	38	128	296	79
Biotech	-22	-323	-401	-334	-348	-370	-397	-378	-489	-382	-344	-216	79	
DOW 30	-1,772	-1,141	334	-1,174	61	-695	401	684	-755	11	1,913	-583	4,066	1,351
DOW 30	-1,772	-2,912	-2,578	-3,752	-3,691	-4,385	-3,984	-3,300	-4,055	-4,045	-2,131	-2,715	1,351	
Finance	-88	-194	-11	-147	-166	98	194	-4	-113	-136	328	61	244	67
Finance	-88	-282	-292	-439	-605	-507	-313	-317	-430	-566	-238	-177	67	
Media	-158	-72	-37	-79	-55	-63	92	3	-42	1	63	48	222	-79
Media	-158	-231	-268	-347	-403	-465	-373	-370	-412	-412	-348	-300	-79	
Technology	-836	-52	148	34	-306	-104	214	-132	-88	126	434	-17	522	-57
Technology	-836	-889	-740	-707	-1,013	-1,117	-902	-1,034	-1,123	-996	-562	-579	-57	
Monthly Sum:	-3,008	-1,832	562	-1,275	-583	-796	911	610	-1,172	113	2,925	-287	5,411	1,577
Acc Sum:	-3,008	-4,841	-4,279	-5,554	-6,137	-6,934	-6,022	-5,413	-6,584	-6,471	-3,546	-3,834	1,577	

1. Create a document with *Portfolio Name*, *Trans Date*, and *Revenue/Expense*
2. Create an xtab with the dates in the rows (column headers) position.
3. Place a break on the *Portfolio Name* column
4. Modify the Trans date row to the following

     = LastDayOfMonth(<Trans Date>)

5. Format the Trans Date row using the Format Cell dialog

     Mmm YY

6. Modify the Revenue/Expense formula to the following

     = <Revenue/Expense> / 1000

7. Select Data->Calculations->Sum from the menu
8. Modify the sum formula in the break footer, (-158) for Media, to

     = RunningSum(<Revenue/Expense>; <Portfolio Name>) / 1000

9. Insert another report footer row and enter the following

     = RunningSum(<Revenue/Expense>) / 1000

10. Delete the unnecessary right-edge sum column
11. Modify the headers

With this report you can ask, "Who was the first to show positive return?", "Who had positive cash the most months?", "Which portfolios had the most risk?"

- In this example, we use the MonthsBetween and the Fill function to create an in-line chart of how many months have past since a contact was last contacted.

Call Port Mgr Name	Call Contact Name	Last Call Date	Months Since Last Call
Kathy James	Thomas O. Staggs	7/7/2000	12 ************
	Jeffrey Mallett	7/13/2000	11 ***********
	Mel Karmazin	12/29/2000	6 ******
	Michael D. Eisner	12/22/2000	6 ******
	Robert A. Iger	12/22/2000	6 ******
	Terry S. Semel	12/19/2000	6 ******
	Richard J. Bressler	4/4/2001	3 ***
	Case, Steve	5/21/2001	1 *
	Kelly, Mike	5/21/2001	1 *
	Sumner M. Redstone	7/7/2001	0

1. Create a document with *Call Port Mgr Name*, *Call Contact Name*, and *Call Date*. Use the following condition
   - Drag the Call Date object to the Conditions window
   - Double-click Less Than or Equal to
   - Double-click Type a new Prompt and enter: Enter Call Date:
2. Run the report and enter 7/7/01, into the prompt dialog.
3. Modify the *Call Date* header to *Last Call Date;* the column formula to
   = Max(<Call Date>)
4. Insert a break on Call Port Mgr Name and delete the footer row for each break.
5. Create a variable
   Name: CurrentDate
   Formula: =ToDate(
       UserResponse(DataProvider(<Call Contact Name>) ,
       "Enter Call Date:") ,"m/d/yy")
6. Insert two columns to the right of *Last Call Date*
7. In the first column enter the following formula
   MonthsBetween(Max(<Call Date>) , <CurrentDate>)
8. In the second column enter the following formula
   =Fill("*", MonthsBetween(Max(<Call Date>), <CurrentDate>))
9. Delete the rightmost header cell and stretch the last header cell across both columns. Then enter the following header
   Months Since Last Call

Logical Functions

- Logical functions return a true or false. They are rarely used by themselves and almost always are used in If-then logic, filters, or hiding report elements
- Probably the two most common are
  - IsNull, is used to test if a value is empty
    If IsNull(<variable>) Then 0 Else <variable>
    - This statement checks if a variable is NULL. If it is, then it replaces the NULL value with a zero. If it is not, then it uses the variable value.
  - IsError, is used to test if a variable is an error
    If IsError(<variable>) Then 0 Else <variable>
    - This statement checks if a variable is an error, such as divide-by-zero. If it is in error, then it uses a zero. If it is not, then it uses the variable.

244

Document Functions

- Documents functions return information about a document.
- The most commonly used are
  - DrillFilters, displays the drill path that has been taken in a report.
  - GlobalFilters, displays any global filters that have been placed on a report. It will not display the filters that have been placed on individual blocks (tables, xtab's, charts).
  - DocumentPartiallyRefreshed, this function is very important, because it will return true if a document is partially refreshed.
    - If DocumentPartiallyRefreshed() Then "Warning - Partially Refreshed!" Once a document is printed, it is very hard to determine if a document has been successfully refreshed. Therefore, it is a good idea to include this function somewhere on most of your reports.
  - Page and NumberOfPages, returns the current page number and the number of pages in a report.
    - Page() + " of " + NumberOfPages()

245

Data Provider Functions

- Data Provider functions return information about the data providers in a document.
- Almost every Data Provider function takes the name of a data provider has the first argument. Most data provider names are similar to *Query 1 with ....*
    - It is better to replace the name with the DataProvider function
        - DataProvider(<AnyObjectFromTheProvider>)
- Examples of Data Provider functions are
    - LastExecutionDate(DataProvider(<obj>))
        - Can be used as Last Refresh Date or As Of Date
    - UserResponse(DataProvider(<obj>), "Prompt Text")
        - Returns the user response to a prompt

Slide 246

1. Create a document with *Portfolio Company, Trans Year, Trans Quarter, Num Transactions*, and *Revenue/Expense.* Place the *Portfolio Names* condition in the Conditions window. Click Run and select any portfolio.

2. Move the Report title to the left side of the report and enter

    = UserResponse(DataProvider(<Portfolio Company>) ,"Please select portfolio names:") + " Companies and Quarterly Report"

3. Insert a cell under the title cell and enter

    ="As of " + FormatDate(LastExecutionDate(DataProvider(<Portfolio Company>)) , "Mmm dd yyyy")

4. Place a break on Portfolio Company and place sums on Num Transactions and Revenue/Expense

Technology Companies and Quarterly Report				
As of Oct 06 2004				

Portfolio Company	Trans Year	Trans Quarter	Num Transactions	Revenue/ Expense
Advanced Micro Devices, Inc.	2000	3	1	-39,954
	2000	4	5	-16,494
	2001	1	2	22,365
	2001	2	3	22,533
	2001	3	1	4,228
Advanced Micro Devices, Inc.		Sum:	12	-7,322

246

Miscellaneous Functions

- Miscellaneous functions do not fit into any of the groups discussed so far.
- Examples are
  - MultiCube, used to synchronize measures through indirect dimension links in multiple data provider documents. There is a good example of this function in the Document Data chapter of this course.
  - NoFilter, this function removes the affects of filters on an object in a report.
  - Previous, allows a formula to reference the value of an object in the previous row of a report.

Trans Year	Trans Week	DOW 30 Transactions	Two-week Moving Avg	Acc DOW 30	% Total Transactions
2000	2	113		113	53.81 %
2000	3	146	130	259	55.22 %
2000	4	145	146	404	55.12 %
2000	5	129	137	533	54.33 %
2000	6	142	136	675	55.10 %
2001	2	135	139	810	55.82 %
2001	3	176	156	986	56.38 %
2001	4	154	165	1,140	56.21 %
2001	5	147	151	1,287	56.08 %
2001	6	204	176	1,491	55.63 %

1. Create a document with *Portfolio Name*, *Trans Year, Trans Week,* and *Num Transactions*

2. Place a filter on Portfolio Name equal to DOW 30

3. Delete the Portfolio Name column, but not the filter

4. Insert three columns to the right of Num Transactions

5. Enter the following into the first inserted column

   = If Not IsNull(Previous(<Num Transactions>)) Then
       (<Num Transactions> + Previous(<Num Transactions>))/2

6. Enter the following into the next column

   = RunningSum(<Num Transactions>)

7. Enter the following into the last column

   = RunningSum(<Num Transactions>) /
       NoFilter(RunningSum(<Num Transactions>))

8. Modify the column headers as they are in the report in the slide

- If-Then-Else allows us to use a logical statement as a switch.
  - If the statement is true, use the Then value
  - If it is false, use the Else value
  - If <True> Then use x Else use y
- An If-Then statement with no Else will either return the *true* value or a NULL
  - (If <True> Then x) is the same as (If <True> Then x Else NULL)
- If-Then-Else statements can be *daisy-chained*
  - If <Month> = 1 Then "January" Else
    If <Month> = 2 Then "February" Else
    ...
    If <Month> = 11 Then "November" Else
    December

Month Name from Month Number

1. Create a document with *Portfolio Name, Trans Year, Trans Month,* and *Revenue/Expense.* Place the condition *Trans Quarter* = 1
2. Modify the Trans Month formula to

   = If <Trans Month> = 1 Then "January" Else If <Trans Month> = 2 Then "February" Else "March"

Easier Method

1. Same as 1, above.
2. Modify the Trans Month formula to

   = ToDate(<Trans Month> + "/1/2004" , "m/d/yyyy")
3. Select any of the dates and select <u>Format->Cell...</u> from the menu
4. On the Number tab, select Date/Time and enter Mmmm into the Date/Time format field

Both of the above methods will display the full month name from a number representation of a month.

Advanced Course for BusinessObjects Reporter

Query Techniques

Introduction

- Most of our reports usually utilize the Query Panel to create our data providers. In this chapter we are going to discuss various methods to create the query that will return the desired data to our documents
  - We will discuss combination queries
    - Union, Intersect, and Minus
  - We are going to use the subquery operand in several examples
  - We will explore the Calculation operand
  - We will even combine the Calculation operand with the subquery operand to create a seemingly complex query

- BusinessObjects allows us to create three different types of combination queries. Each of these can only combine data from a single data provider. In the Venn diagrams below, the lighter color represents the data that is returned
  - Union Queries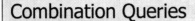
    Use to combine similar sets of data.
  - Intersect Queries
    Use to intersect similar sets of data.
  - Minus Queries
    Use to subtract a similar set of data from another.

Combination queries are used to logically relate two sets of data. We can union, intersect, or minus the sets. BusinessObjects allows us to perform combination queries on sets of data created in a single data provider.

- Union Queries combine the results of two different queries, from the same data provider, by concatenating the results of one to the other.
- Since the sets are concatenated, both sets of data must have the same number of columns, the same types of columns, and in the same order.

Portfolio Name	Trans Date	Revenue/Expense
Alternative Energy	7/14/2000	-10,318.00
Alternative Energy	7/18/2000	-5,325.00

Portfolio Name	Trans Date	Revenue/Expense
Alternative Energy	7/14/2000	-10,318.00
Alternative Energy	7/18/2000	-5,325.00

⇩ ⇩ ⇩   ⇩ Ⓝ ⇩

Portfolio Name	Trans Date	Revenue/Expense
DOW 30	7/14/2000	-131,375.00
DOW 30	7/18/2000	-142,875.00

Portfolio Name	Trans Month	Revenue/Expense
DOW 30	7	-274,250.00

Portfolio Name	Trans Date	Revenue/Expense
Alternative Energy	7/14/2000	-10,318.00
Alternative Energy	7/18/2000	-5,325.00
DOW 30	7/14/2000	-131,375.00
DOW 30	7/18/2000	-142,875.00

Union queries concatenate two sets of data from the same data provider. Union queries are often used to concatenate queries from two different contexts. They are also often used to concatenate data from the same context, but with different logical conditions.

Union queries are fast and efficient. Most databases perform union queries locally, thus eliminating the need for BusinessObjects to manage the data. This means that BusinessObjects sends a union query to the database and it returns one unified set of data.

Therefore, once the data is returned to the document, it may be impossible to determine which query in the union returned a specific row. If this identification is needed, the report developer will usually place an object in each query that will uniquely identify the query from where the row came.

Since, the number, type, and order of columns must match in the queries, it may be necessary to include a NULL space holder for a column in one of the queries. Not all universes have these NULL objects, but it is highly recommended that they do. The SI EQUITY universe has these NULL objects.

252

Union Query Example

- Suppose that we had a manager switch portfolios after the first year. However, we need to get his/her two year total. We can use a union query to combine the first year results to the second year results.

- In the example below, our manager worked in Biotech in 2000 and in Technology in 2001.

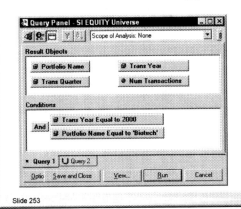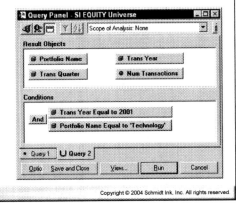

1. Create a document with *Portfolio Name*, *Trans Year*, *Trans Quarter*, and *Num Transactions*. Place the following conditions

   Trans Year = 2000

   Portfolio Name = Biotech

2. Click the <u>Combine Queries</u> button in the Query Panel

   Notice that the same objects occupy the <u>Result Objects</u> window, but the conditions are not duplicated. The redundant Result Objects are to remind you that the objects must match the first query's objects in type, number, and order.

3. Place the following conditions

   Trans Year = 2001

   Portfolio Name = Technology

4. Click the Run button.

- Intersect queries only return the rows that are in common to both sets of data. The values must match in value, type, and order.
- Intersect queries have the same rules as union queries, both sets of data must have the same number of columns, the same types of columns, and in the same order.
  - In addition to these rules, one must consider that as more columns are to be intersected, the less probability for an intersection.
    - For example, if we divide the room into guys and gals
      - It will be probable that there are brown haired people in both
      - Less probable, if we add that they must be over 5' 5"
      - Even less probable, if we add that they should have blue eyes

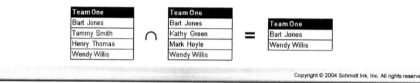

Intersect queries do allow us to intersect two queries. However, there use is limited, since the more columns we add - the less likely we are to get an intersection. Later, in this chapter, we will learn how to use a subquery to return the same information, but in more detail.

Intersect Query Example

- Suppose our task is to determine which DOW 30 portfolio companies are also traded in the Technology portfolio
- We can use an Intersect query to intersect the list of DOW 30 companies with the list of Technology companies
  - This example will determine which DOW 30 companies are also traded in Technology. However, because of the limitations mentioned in the previous slide, it is probably better to use a subquery to achieve the same results.

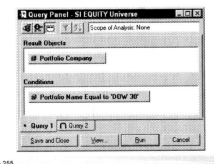 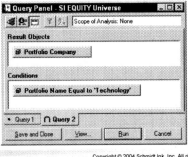

1. Create a document with *Portfolio Company*. Place the following condition

   Portfolio Name = DOW 30

2. Click the <u>Combine Queries</u> button in the Query Panel

   Notice that the symbol on the tab of the second query is a U. The U stands for union query, which is the default combination query.

   To change it to an ∩, double-click on the U.

3. Place the following condition

   Portfolio Name = Technology

4. Click the Run button.

Minus Query

- Minus queries remove rows from a query, where they exactly match rows in a second query.
- Minus queries have the same rules as Intersect and Union queries. However, since the query subtracts the rows that are in common to the first query, order matters.
  - A U B = B U A, and A ∩ B = B ∩ A. However, A – B ≠ B - A

256

Minus Query Example

- Suppose we want to know what dates the portfolio manager made calls, but made no transactions?
- We can do this by making a query with all of the call dates and then subtract the dates that are in common to the set of all transactions.

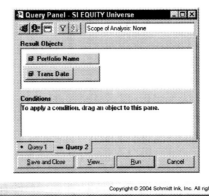

1. Create a document with *Call Portfolio Name* and *Call Date.*

2. Click the <u>Combine Queries</u> button in the Query Panel

   Notice that the symbol on the tab of the second query is a U. The U stands for union query, which is the default combination query. To change it to a minus (-), double-click on the U two times.

3. Remove both objects from the query and then place *Portfolio Name* and *Trans Date* in the <u>Result Objects</u> window

4. Click the Run button.

Combination Queries Vs. Subqueries

- Of the three combination queries, two of them can usually be replaced with a subquery, which is more efficient and less restrictive.
    - These two combinations are Intersect and Minus. Subqueries allow us to Intersect a single column, or minus rows based on a single column.
        - Since, we are using a single column for the comparison and not the entire row, we can add information that would not be allowed in the combination query.
- The Union query is the concatenation of two sets of data and therefore, cannot be replaced with a subquery that only constricts the amount of data returned to a document.

258

The In List Operator

- The condition below, will return rows to a query where Portfolio Ticker is BORL, AMD,AMAT or BOBJ.

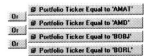

- The above condition will indeed return the desired results. However, since each condition is Or'ed together, it gets very awkward as more conditions are added. The condition below, will return the same rows. However, it uses the InList operator and a list of values for an operand.
  - The list of values is easier to expand.
  - The InList operator makes the condition easier to work with, because the list is contained in a single condition statement

> ☑ Portfolio Ticker In list 'AMAT,AMD,BOBJ,BORL'

259

List of Values Vs. Subqueries

- Many times a static list of values is what is needed for a condition.
  - Year InList 2000, 2001
  - Portfolio Name InList DOW 30, Alternative Energy, Media
- Subqueries create a dynamic list of values. In addition, this list as virtually no limitations on the number of entries.
- This query returns a list of all Portfolio Companies in the Technology portfolio

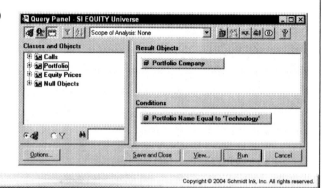

Using a list of values in the operand of a condition is great for hard-coded static values, such as years, states, or regions. However, if the list is dynamic and based on criteria within the database, it is very convenient to use a subquery to define the list.

Intersect Query Using Subquery

- Earlier, we used the Intersection query to discover which DOW 30 companies were also traded in the Technology portfolio. In this example, we will use a subquery to retrieve the same information, plus a little more.

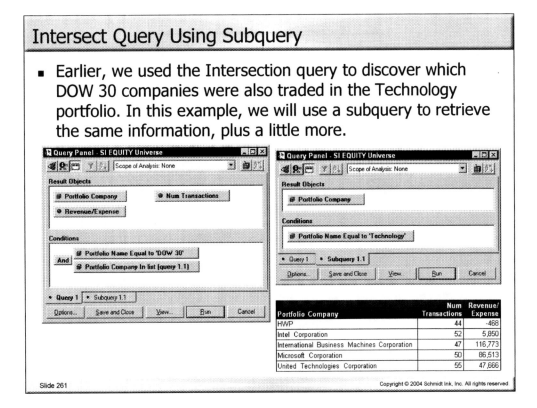

1. Create a query with *Portfolio Company*, *Num Transactions* and *Revenue/Expense*
2. Create a condition *Portfolio Name* equal to DOW 30
3. Drag the *Portfolio Company* object from the <u>Classes and Objects</u> window and drop it in the <u>Conditions</u> window
4. Select the InList operator from the <u>Operators</u> window
5. Double-click on the Create a Subquery operand
6. In the Subquery panel, Drag the *Portfolio Company* object to the <u>Result Objects</u> window
7. Place a condition *Portfolio Name* equal to Technology.
8. Activate the outer query (Query 1) and make sure that the two conditions are Or'ed together
9. Click the Run button.

Since the outer query's columns don't have to match the subquery's columns, as in the Intersect query, we are able to retrieve much more information.

- Earlier, we used a minus query to determine the portfolios and dates that made calls, but no trades.
- We will not be able to create the same query with a subquery, because the subquery only uses one column for comparison. However, if we hold the portfolio constant, we will be able to find the dates that a portfolio made calls, but no transactions.

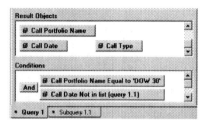

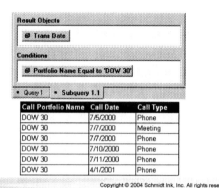

1. Create a query with *Call Portfolio Name*, *Call Date* and *Call Type*

2. Create a condition *Call Portfolio Name* equal to DOW 30

3. Drag the *Call Date* object from the <u>Classes and Objects</u> window and drop it in the <u>Conditions</u> window

4. Select the Not InList operator from the <u>Operators</u> window

5. Double-click on the Create a Subquery operand

6. In the Subquery panel, Drag the *Trans Date* object to the <u>Result Objects</u> window

7. Place a condition *Portfolio Name* equal to DOW 30.

8. Activate the outer query (Query 1) and make sure that the two conditions are And'ed together

9. Click the Run button.

In this example we find the dates that the DOW 30 portfolio made calls, but no transactions. The minus query allowed us to do all portfolios at one time, but limited the information retrieved to Portfolio Names and Call Dates.

Other Subquery Uses

- Subqueries can can be used return detail information using a summary condition
    - We can return the companies that generated more than $100,000. We can also return the trade dates, the portfolio names and, the number of transactions
- Subqueries also allow us to circumvent pre-established joins and contexts in a universe.
    - For example, suppose we wanted to know the closing prices and volumes for all of the equities in the Alternative Energy Portfolio. This query needs information from two different contexts in the SI Equity universe.

263

- In this example, we want to show the transaction details for the equities in our portfolios that generated more than $100,000 for the life of the fund.
- To do this, we will create a query with all of the details that we want to examine. This query will use a subquery to limit the equities to the companies that generated $100,000 or more.

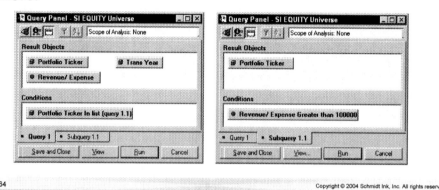

1. Create a query with *Portfolio Ticker*, *Trans Year*, and *Revenue/Expense*
2. Create the subquery condition by dragging *Portfolio Ticker* from the Classes and Objects window to the Conditions window
3. Double-click the In list operator
4. Double-click the Create a subquery operator
5. On the subquery tab, place *Portfolio Ticker* in the Result Objects window
6. Drag the *Revenue/Expense* object to the Conditions window
7. Double-click the Greater than operator
8. Double-click the Type a new constant operand and type 100000
9. Click the Run button

- Running this query will return detail information for the Portfolio Tickers that generated more than $100,000.
- Other examples of detail information from a summary subquery include, but are definitely not limited to
  - Finding out who your top sales people are and who they sold products to.
  - Determining what instruments your top brokers are selling.
  - Returning the products that are sold in your most productive cities and a list of who is buying the products.

Portfolio Ticker	Trans Year	Revenue/ Expense
AA	2000	-259,238
	2001	432,050
AA	Sum:	172,813
IBM	2000	-567,825
	2001	698,848
IBM	Sum:	131,023
MMM	2000	-380,363
	2001	577,350
MMM	Sum:	196,988

- Suppose you want to know the closing prices for all of the stocks in a certain portfolio? This is difficult, because the closing prices are in a different context than the portfolio equities.

- The solution is to use a subquery to return a list of equities that are contained in a portfolio. A main query will use this list to limit the equities retuned by the main query.

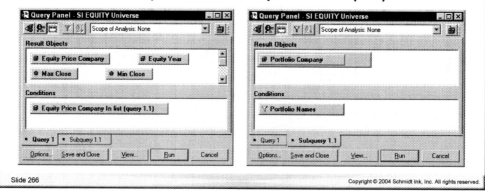

1. Create a query with *Equity Price Company*, *Equity Year*, *Max Close* and *Min Close*

2. Create the subquery condition by dragging *Equity Price Company* from the Classes and Objects window to the Conditions window

3. Double-click the In list operator

4. Double-click the Create a subquery operand

5. On the subquery tab, place *Portfolio Company* in the Result Objects window

6. Drag the *Portfolio Names* condition to the Conditions window

7. Click the Run button

8. Select any Portfolio Name from the prompt dialog

- In this example we used a list of Portfolio Company Names from the Portfolio context to limit the companies in a query that returns the Max Close and Min Close for each company in the portfolio list.

Equity Price Company	Equity Year	Max Close	Min Close	Max - Min	% Move
AOL Time Warner Inc.	2000	63.00	34.80	28.20	81 %
AOL Time Warner Inc.	2001	56.60	32.39	24.21	75 %
Fox Entertainment Group, Inc.	2000	33.00	15.81	17.19	109 %
Fox Entertainment Group, Inc.	2001	29.28	17.88	11.41	64 %
Viacom Inc.	2000	74.63	44.94	29.69	66 %
Viacom Inc.	2001	59.58	39.79	19.79	50 %
Walt Disney Company	2000	42.50	26.44	16.06	61 %
Walt Disney Company	2001	34.50	26.91	7.59	28 %
Yahoo! Inc.	2000	139.81	25.63	114.19	446 %
Yahoo! Inc.	2001	42.88	11.38	31.50	277 %

1. Insert two columns to the right of *Min Close*

2. Insert the following formula into the first inserted column

    = <Max Close> - <Min Close>

3. Label the column

    Max - Min

4. Insert the following formula into the second inserted column

    = (<Max Close> - <Min Close>) / <Min Close>

5. Label the column

    % Move

- So far, all of our subqueries have used the In List operator. This cause a subquery to do a simple in list comparison.
- If we were to use a logical operator, such as Equal to, Greater than, Less than, and so forth, then we would have to choose from Subquery All or Subquery Any.
  - Subquery All, means that for a row to return, the condition would have to be true for all values returned by the subquery
  - Subquery Any, means that the condition will only have to be true for one value returned by the subquery.

Subqueries that work with the all and any keywords allow users to state conditions that are true for all values in a list or any value in a list.

For example, the In list operator allowed us to return a row if the value in the row was in the list created by the subquery. The Equal to operator will have the same results if we created a subquery that was true for any value in the list. Therefore,

- In List - Create a subquery

Is equivalent to

- Equal to - Create a subquery (Any)

The **Greater than or equal to - Create a subquery (All)** or the **Less Than or equal to - Create a subquery (All)** combinations are usually used to find maximums or minimum, respectively.

- There is a new operand type in version 6.x, that allows you to use objects in another query, in the document, as a list of values in your operand. This operand is Select Query Results.
    - This means that you can create lists from universes, text files, MS Excel files, VBA, or one of the many other data provider types.

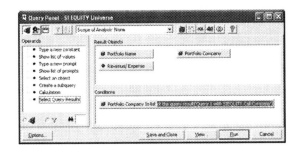

The Select Query Results is a very powerful operand that allows you to use the values of an object in another query, in the same document. This is a very exciting new feature and just may be the one single important enough reason to upgrade from version 5.x.

1. Select *File>New...* from the menu.
2. Create a new query with Call Company, Call Portfolio Name, and Num Calls. Click Run.
3. Right-click on the Report Manager and select New Data Provider.
4. Select Build a new query on the universe currently in use. Click Finish
5. Select Portfolio Name, Portfolio Company, and Revenue/Expense.
6. Drag Portfolio Company from the Classes and Objects window to the Conditions window.
7. Double-click the In List operator,
8. Double-click the Select Query Results operand.
9. Select Call Company in Query 1 with SIEQUITY and click OK.
10. Click Run.
11. Drag Revenue/Expense and drop it beside Num Calls.
12. Select *Data>View Data...* and link the dimension values.

269

- In this example, we are going to create a query that returns the top five Portfolio Companies, and then use the results from that query as a list that will return the details of the transactions of the top five Portfolio Companies.
  - This type of query was nearly impossible in BusinessObjects versions four and five.

Portfolio Company	Portfolio Industry	Trans Quarter	Trans Year	Revenue/ Expense
Alcoa Inc.	Metals	1	2001	-133,488
	Metals	2	2001	246,958
	Metals	3	2000	-99,338
	Metals	3	2001	318,598
	Metals	4	2000	-199,900
Alcoa Inc.			Sum:	173,813
Caterpillar Inc.	Industrial	1	2001	-186,225
	Industrial	2	2001	247,259
	Industrial	3	2000	-98,900
	Industrial	3	2001	89,860
	Industrial	4	2000	-14,163
Caterpillar Inc.			Sum:	97,823
International Business Machines Corporation	Technology	1	2001	385,875
	Technology	2	2001	253,173
	Technology	3	2000	-48,553
	Technology	3	2001	99,803
	Technology	4	2000	-618,275
International Business Machines Corporation			Sum:	131,023
Microsoft Corporation	Technology	1	2001	30,869
	Technology	2	2001	269,155
	Technology	3	2000	-266,194
	Technology	3	2001	150,599
	Technology	4	2000	-92,935
Microsoft Corporation			Sum:	99,495
Minnesota Mining and Manufacturing Company	Industrial	1	2001	341,875
	Industrial	2	2001	-110,488
	Industrial	3	2000	-138,013
	Industrial	3	2001	345,963
	Industrial	4	2000	-242,350
Minnesota Mining and Manufacturing Company			Sum:	196,988

1. Select *File>New…* from the menu.

2. Place Portfolio Company and Revenue/Expense from the Portfolio class, into the Results Objects window.

3. Click the Options button in the Query Panel, select the Other option in the Partial Results section, and enter 5 into the edit field. Click OK.

4. Select the Revenue/Expense object in the Result Objects window, and click the Sort toolbar button on the left side of the panel. Double-click on the sort icon that is now on the Revenue/Expense object . This will make it sort Z to A.

5. Click Run. (This will return the top five companies)

6. Select *Data>New Data Provider…* from the menu. Leave the Build a new query on the universe currently in use option selected and click Finish.

7. Select Portfolio Company, Portfolio Industry, Trans Year, Trans Quarter, and Revenue/Expense from the Portfolio class.

8. Drag the Portfolio Company object from the Classes and Objects window into the Conditions window.

9. Double-click the In List operator.

10. Double-click the Select Query Results operand, select Portfolio Company from Query 1, and then click OK. Click Run.

11. Select *Insert>Report* from the menu.

12. Drag the objects from the new query onto the new report and format the report.

270

Eliminating Double Counts on Shared Values

- Many companies have potential for double counting measures.
  - In some investment banks, several departments may claim the revenue from a certain deal. This means that the details will be correct. However, when you some the rows, the total will be multiplied by the number of departments claiming credit.
  - Some tech departments have Case Id's and Solution Id's. A single case can have multiple solutions. Therefore, when solutions are combined with cases, the solutions multiply the number of cases.
- There are many ways around this type of error. In this class we will discuss two.

1. Select *File>New...* from the menu.

2. Create a query with Call Portfolio Name, Call Company, Call Port Mgr Name, Call Contact Name, Call Id and, Num Calls. (Some of these objects came from the Multiple folder, because they will cause a double count when added to the query. This is because on a single call there can be several portfolio managers and several company contacts)

3. Click Run.

4. Delete the Call ID column, so the calls will total for each row. (Since several managers and contacts can be on a single call, a call can be shared by several different rows in the table)

5. Place a break on Call Portfolio Name.

6. Sum Num Calls. (These sums can be greatly skewed, if several managers and contacts are sharing single calls)

7. Click on the word Sum in the footer and select *Data>Edit Formula...*

8. Enter
= Count(<Call Id>), and click OK. (Notice that the true number of calls for Biotech is actually 23 and not 37)

Use Existing Query to Eliminate Double Counts (V6.x)

- There is a new feature in version 6.x that makes it very convenient to copy existing queries.
- This is the 'Use existing query to build a new one' option when inserting a new data provider.

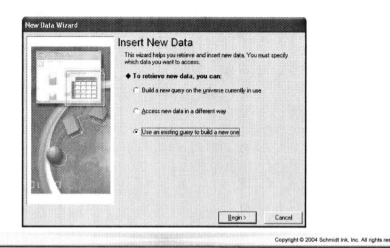

1. Select *File>New...* from the menu.

2. Create a query with Call Portfolio Name, Call Company, Call Port Mgr Name, Call Contact Name, and Num Calls. (Notice that we did not bring in Call ID, as we did in the previous example. This allows us to retrieve summary information and not bring back detail information on every call)

3. Click Run.

4. Place a break on Call Portfolio Name.

5. Sum Num Calls. (Due to double counts, this sum will be too large)

6. Right-click in the Report Manager and select *New Data Provider...*

7. Select the *Use existing query to build a new one* option and click Finish.

8. Remove the objects that will cause a multiple count and click Run. (Call Port Man Name and Call Contact Name. Technically, Call Portfolio Name will also cause a multiple count, but since we are totaling within the Portfolio break, it is of no matter)

9. Click the View Data button and rename the queries to Detail and summary, respectively.

10. Drag Num Call (Summary) to just beside Num Call (Detail)

11. Also drag it to the footer cell.

12. Change the column formula to: =<Num Calls(Detail)>/<Num Calls(Summary)>, and format it to percent.

272

Calculation Condition Operands

- Calculation operands create calculated subqueries
  - These subqueries create a list of calculated values based on a measure's default aggregate or an aggregated dimension
  - The list can contain one value, calculated globally; or the list can contain more values, aggregated to one or more dimensions
  - The list of values entries can even be synchronized to dimensions in the Result Objects window

Calculation Operand Example and Explanation

- Let's do an example that uses the Calculation Operand Wizard and discuss every step of the wizard as we go.
- In this example, we will determine the date that our company spent the most money buying equities.

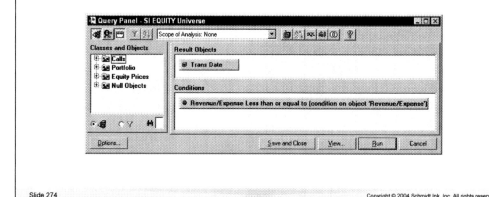

1. Create a query with *Trans Date*
2. Drag *Revenue/Expense* from the Classes and Objects window to the Conditions window
3. Double-click the Less than or equal to operator
4. Double-click the Calculation operand

Step One: Select an Object

- The first step of the calculation allows us to select an object to use in our calculation
  - If we choose a dimension, the next step will be for us to choose an aggregate function
  - If we choose a measure, the wizard will not allow us to select an aggregate function, since measures already have a default function

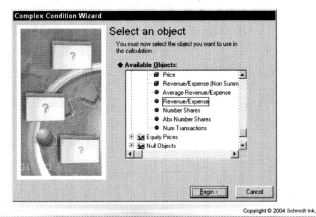

1. Select the Revenue/Expense object
2. Click the Begin > button to go to the next step

We chose Revenue/Expense, because we are interested in returning a list of all Revenue/Expense values. We will not choose an aggregate function, because the Revenue/Expense measure already has the sum aggregation function.

In older versions of BusinessObjects, the wizard would allow an aggregation function to be selected, even for a measure. This assignment would cause an SQL error, because in SQL you cannot aggregate an aggregate.

275

- The Calculation operand will return a list of values
  - If the Globally option is selected, it will return one value aggregated across all rows in the data set
  - If By one or more objects is selected, than the list will be aggregated to the chosen dimensions

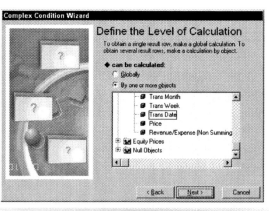

1. Select the By one or more objects option
2. Select the Trans Year object
3. Click the Next > button to go to the next step

We chose By one or more objects, because we want to return a list of Revenue/Expense aggregated to the Trans Date dimension. This means that the calculation list will contain a list with as many values as there are unique Trans Dates.

Step Three: Synchronize Your Calculation

- Sometimes we want the values in the list to be limited to the values generated by each unique value of a dimension in our Result Objects window
    - The For each value of one or more objects option allows the list to be synchronized
        - If this option is chosen, then the query may, and probably will, take a substantial amount of time to execute
    - Independently of your objects, causes the list to be generated with no regard to the values of the dimensions in the Result Objects window

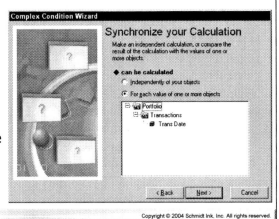

1. Select the Independently of your objects option
2. Click the Next > button to go to the next step

We chose the Independently of your objects option, because we want to return a list of revenues for each date in the data provider. We we needed a different list for each value of a dimension in the Result Objects window, then we would have to synchronize the the list. This is known as a correlated subquery to SQL programmers. It is correlated, because the list is regenerated for each value of the synchronized object. This means that the list can be generated hundred's of times, which will cause the query to take very long to execute.

Step Four: Set the Number of Values to Compare

- The calculation operand will return a list of values to the condition. Then the condition statement can either be true for one value or all values in the list
    - At least one value, as soon as one value causes the condition to be true, the entire condition is accepted
    - All values, the condition must be true for all values in the list

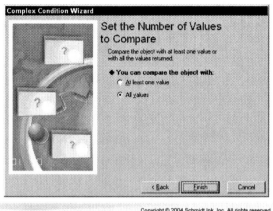

1. Select the All values option
2. Click the Finish button to accept the operand settings
3. Click Run to execute the query

We chose the All values option, because we want to find the revenue/expense that is less than or equal to every value in the revenue/expense list returned by the calculation operand.

If all of the settings are correctly set, the report will return a value of 7/26/04, which is the date that the company spent the most money trading.

Calculation Operand Combined with a Subquery

- In the previous example, we had only the Trans Date object in the Result Objects window. If we were to add any more dimension objects, the query would probably return no values, because the extra dimensions will cause the Revenue/Expenses to diffuse among the other dimension values. In this example, we will use the same calculation in a subquery.

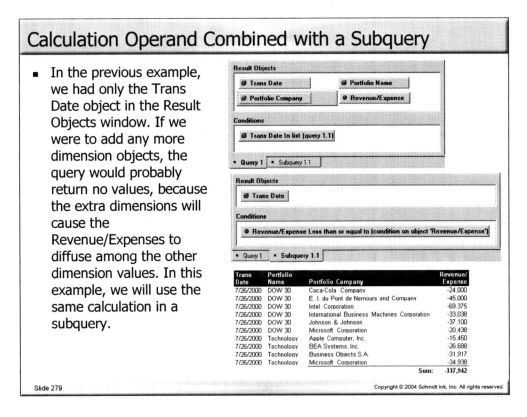

1. Create a query with *Trans Date*, *Portfolio Name*, *Portfolio Company*, and *Revenue/Expense*

2. Drag the Trans Date object from the Classes and Objects window to the Conditions window

3. Choose the In List operator

4. Double-click the Create a Subquery operand

5. On the Subquery tab, drag the Trans Date object to the Result Objects window

6. Drag the Revenue/Expense object to the Conditions window

7. Double-click the Less than or equal to operator

8. Double- click the Calculation operand

   1. Select the Revenue/Expense object

   2. Select Trans Date as the Level of Calculation

   3. Select Independently of your objects on Synchronization

   4. Select All Values for Number of values to compare

   5. Click Finish

9. Click Run

279

Advanced Course for BusinessObjects Reporter

Formatting Reports

Introduction

- Once we have the data and formulas that we need to create our reports, we need to format the report into a powerful presentation. In this chapter we are going to
  - How to manipulate rows and columns
  - Create space saving reports
  - Prevent a report from aggregating
  - Make column reports
  - Hide sections and blocks
  - Format crosstabs

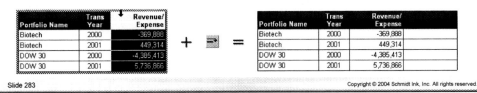

Inserting Rows and Columns

- To insert a row, select a cell in a block and then click the Insert Row Below or Insert Row Above button in the Report Toolbar.

Portfolio Name	Trans Year	Revenue/ Expense
Biotech	2000	-369,888
Biotech	2001	449,314
DOW 30	2000	-4,385,413
DOW 30	2001	5,736,866

+ ⬛ =

Portfolio Name	Trans Year	Revenue/ Expense
Biotech	2000	-369,888
Biotech	2001	449,314
DOW 30	2000	-4,385,413
DOW 30	2001	5,736,866

- To insert a column, select any cell in the column that you desire to be adjacent to your new column and then select Insert->Column... from the menu.

Portfolio Name	Trans Year	Revenue/ Expense
Biotech	2000	-369,888
Biotech	2001	449,314
DOW 30	2000	-4,385,413
DOW 30	2001	5,736,866

+ ⬛ =

Portfolio Name	Trans Year	Revenue/ Expense	
Biotech	2000	-369,888	
Biotech	2001	449,314	
DOW 30	2000	-4,385,413	
DOW 30	2001	5,736,866	

Slide 283

Rows

Users can insert rows into the details of a block, as shown above, or into the headers or footers of blocks. A partial row can not be inserted. Therefore, any cell in a row or the entire row can be selected before a row is inserted into a block.

Columns

BusinessObjects will allow you to insert a partial column into a document. You do this by first selecting a partial column and then by clicking the Insert Cell button, not the Insert Column button.

Dragging Cells: On a Report

- Users can drag cells to other locations on a report. They can drag cells to other cells within the same block, to other blocks or to anywhere on a report
- To drag a cell, click on it once to select it, then click again, hold the left-mouse button down and drag the cell to a new location. Then simply release the mouse button
- Examples of dragging cells on a report
    - Dragging a free standing cell, such as the title of a report

    - Dragging cells within a block or to another block

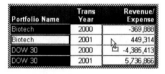

Users may want to drag a free standing cell, such as the title of a report, to reposition it on a report. Users may also want to drag the contents of a populated column to a newly inserted column in a block.

To drag a cell

- Select the cell(s) by clicking on it (them)
- Then click on it again and hold the left-mouse button down. The cursor will change to a drag cursor, as seen in the slide
- Drag the cell to a new location and release the mouse button

Dragging Cells: Switching, Moving and Copying Cells

- We can define the drop behavior of a cell by holding down certain keys before releasing the mouse button.
  - To copy the cells contents, hold down the [Ctrl] key

Portfolio Name	Trans Year	Revenue/ Expense	
Biotech	2000	-369,888	
Biotech	2001	449,314	
DOW 30	2000	-4,385,413	
DOW 30	2001	5,736,866	

  - To move the cell's contents, hold down the [Shift] key

Portfolio Name	Trans Year	Revenue/ Expense	
Biotech	2000	-369,888	
Biotech	2001	449,314	
DOW 30	2000	-4,385,413	
DOW 30	2001	5,736,866	

  - To swap cell contents, hold down no key

Portfolio Name	Trans Year	Revenue/ Expense	
Biotech	2000	-369,888	
Biotech	2001	449,314	
DOW 30	2000	-4,385,413	
DOW 30	2001	5,736,866	

Once users get familiar with using keys as they drag cells on a report, they begin to use this functionality more and more. For example, a user may copy the revenue column to an empty column just to the right of the existing column and alter the formula slightly, maybe by dividing by 1,000. Users also often use this functionality to swap columns on a report.

Remember, cells can be dragged to other blocks on a report or even outside of all blocks and directly on a report.

Note: When cells are dragged and dropped to a new location, regardless of if they are copied, moved or swapped, they will acquire the format of the cell in which they are dropped. To override this behavior and to force the new location to be formatted as the previous location, simply hold the [Alt] key down in addition to the [Ctrl] or [Shift] key.

- Users can drag cells outside of blocks. The behavior of the dropped cell depends on it's type and where it is dropped.
  - A Measure object can be dropped on a free-standing cell or on a report. The measure object will display a calculation based on the entire report, or if the measure is dropped into a section, the section total.

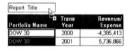

  - A dimension dropped onto a freestanding cell will cause a #Multivalue error. It will probably also cause a #Multivalue error, if the dimension is dropped into a header cell.

Cells in blocks behave differently than free-standing cells on a report. For example, the rows in blocks define distinct combinations of dimension and detail values. Any measures in this block will conform and display calculations for these distinct combinations of values.

When an object or variable is removed from a block and placed in a free standing on a report the values for the object must conform to free-standing cell.

- If the object is a measure, it will simply display the calculation it was designed to perform, such as a sum, minimum, maximum, etc.

- If the object is a dimension or detail, it is not able to expand as it does in a block and a #Multivalue error will be displayed.

Slide 287

Cross Tables

As shown above, a column can be dragged to the upper right-most cell to create a cross table. Once the xtab is created, additional header rows can be added, by dragging an object to the lowermost part of the header, to insert a header row below, or to the uppermost part of the header to insert a row above. Notice that in the example below, the outline for the dropped cell only highlights the bottom half of the header row.

	2000	2001
Biotech	-369,888	449,314
DOW 30	-4,385,413	5,736,866

	2000 3	2000 4	2001 1	2001 2	2001 3
Biotech	-400,996	31,108	-119,552	273,348	295,519
DOW 30	-2,578,025	-1,807,388	330,350	1,340,450	4,066,066

Master Detail

In the previous slide, when we dragged a dimension cell from a block, we received a #Multivalue error. The difference is on that slide we dragged the dimension to an existing cell. In this slide we dropped the dimension object on the report itself.

287

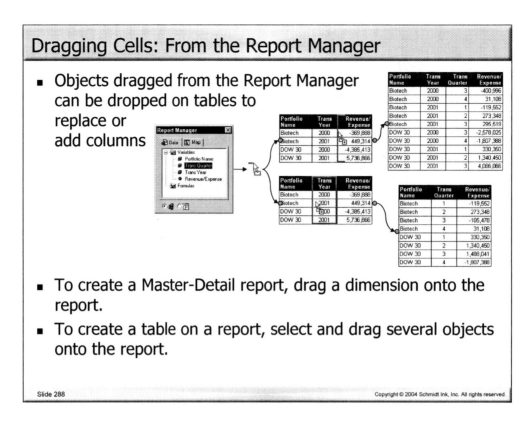

Dragging Cells: From the Report Manager

- Objects dragged from the Report Manager can be dropped on tables to replace or add columns

- To create a Master-Detail report, drag a dimension onto the report.
- To create a table on a report, select and drag several objects onto the report.

Users can use the Report Manager as sort of an object browser, which allows them to drag and drop variables from the Data tab. Users can drag variables to existing blocks on a report and, as shown above, these dropped variables can either replace existing columns or create additional columns.

If the user wants to replace an existing column, the variable is dropped on a column when the entire column is outlined by the drop rectangle. If the user wants the variable to be placed in a new column in the block, the variable is placed to the right or left side of the column it is to be inserted next to. The user then drops the variable when the drop rectangle only covers the right or left portion of the column. Both of these scenarios are illustrated above.

If a users wants t create a Master - Detail report, the user simply drops the dimension variable on the report. This will create sections on the report that represent each value of the variable.

To create a table, select multiple objects in the Report Manager. Then click on the selection and drag it out onto the report.

- Sometimes, our reports are just too wide to fit on a single page width. One reason for this is that there are just too many columns
- In this example, we add extra rows to the body of a report and then consolidate the columns using the extra rows

Portfolio Name	Portfolio Mgr Name	Port Initial Cash	Revenue/ Expense	Number Shares	Num Transactions
Alternative Energy	David Balkcom	275,000	303,886	-10,200	96
Biotech	Maria Castro	525,000	449,314	-9,400	93
DOW 30	Sean Wilkenson	5,000,000	5,736,866	-90,200	816
Finance	Robert Denning	625,000	574,563	-8,700	75
Media	Kathy James	500,000	386,854	-9,400	58
Technology	Eddie Wang	1,250,000	1,059,497	-28,000	317

Portfolio Name	Portfolio Mgr Name	Port Initial Cash
Revenue/ Expense	Number Shares	Num Transactions
Alternative Energy	David Balkcom	275,000
303,886	-10,200	96
Biotech	Maria Castro	525,000
449,314	-9,400	93
DOW 30	Sean Wilkenson	5,000,000
5,736,866	-90,200	816
Finance	Robert Denning	625,000
574,563	-8,700	75
Media	Kathy James	500,000
386,854	-9,400	58
Technology	Eddie Wang	1,250,000
1,059,497	-28,000	317

1. Create a report with *Portfolio Name*, *Portfolio Mgr Name*, *Port Initial Cash*, *Revenue/Expense*, *Number Shares*, and *Num Transactions*
2. Click on a the report and insert two rows below it
3. Click on any header in the report and insert a row below it
4. Drag the three rightmost header cells unto the first three header cells of the newly inserted header row
5. Drag the three rightmost data cells onto the the first three cells of the newly inserted body row
6. Delete the now empty three rightmost columns
7. Highlight the empty row between the records and remove the borders

- Break reports usually only have the break value in the first row of each break and this value does not change for the entire break section.
  - In this example, we will move the break from from the report body to the break header. This will allow the break value to be represented in the report without using a column for the value.

Portfolio Name	Trans Year	Revenue/ Expense	Number Shares	Num Transactions
Alternative Energy	2000	-89,221	10,200	78
	2001	303,886	-10,200	96
Alternative Energy	Sum:	214,665	0	174
Biotech	2000	-369,888	9,400	91
	2001	449,314	-9,400	93
Biotech	Sum:	79,426	0	184

Trans Year	Revenue/ Expense	Number Shares	Num Transactions
Alternative Energy			
2000	-89,221	10,200	78
2001	303,886	-10,200	96
Sum:	214,665	0	174
Biotech			
2000	-369,888	9,400	91
2001	449,314	-9,400	93
Sum:	79,426	0	184

1. Create a report with *Portfolio Name*, *Trans Year*, *Revenue/Expense*, *Number Shares*, and *Num Transactions*
2. Click on the *Portfolio Name* column and insert a break
3. Select <u>Format->Breaks...</u> from the menu
4. Select the Break Header option in the Break Definition section
5. Click OK
6. Drag the Portfolio Name from the body of the break unto the *Trans Year* break header cell (hold the [Ctrl] down, because there may be an error in some BusinessObjects versions
7. Delete the *Portfolio Name* column
8. Delete the three break header cells to the right of the *Portfolio Name*
9. Expand the Portfolio Name cell to the width of the table

    Select the cell, then drag the edge to the width of the table
10. Remove the shading and format as desired

Avoid Duplicate Row Aggregation

- The default behavior of BusinessObjects is to create row contexts out of each unique combination of non-measure object values in a table.
  - For example, even if this table has several rows for Biotech, they will consolidate into one row and the measure will aggregate to the row

Portfolio Name	Num Transactions
Biotech	184
DOW 30	1,491
Finance	120

- If you need to see each row value in a table, before it is aggregated, then use the Avoid Duplicate Row Aggregation option on the General tab of the Block Format dialog

Portfolio Name	Num Transactions
Biotech	91
Biotech	93
DOW 30	675
DOW 30	816
Finance	45
Finance	75

1. Create a report with *Portfolio Name*, *Trans Year*, and *Num Transactions*
2. Delete the Trans Year Column, so that the Num Transactions will re-aggregate to each Portfolio Name
3. Click anywhere on the table and select Format->Table… from the menu
4. Click the General tab to activate it
5. Select the Avoid Duplicate Rows Aggregation option
6. Click OK

It seems strange that we may want to use this option. However, it is often used to help debug a report.

291

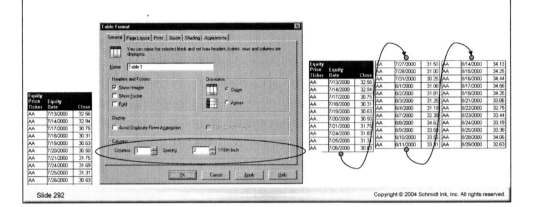

1. Create a report with *Equity Price Ticker*, *Equity Date*, and *Close*
2. Change the Equity Price Ticker header to Ticker
3. Format the columns to be a narrow as possible
4. Select <u>View->Page Layout</u> from the menu

    The option only applies to Page Layout mode, and when the report is printed

5. Click anywhere on the table and select <u>Format->Table...</u> from the menu
6. Enter a 4 in the <u>Columns</u> option and a 1 in the <u>Spacing</u> option

    You could enter 100 in the Columns option, but BusinessObjects will only create as many column that will fit on a single page width

7. To further enhance the report, we can set a break on Ticker and start each one a a new page

    1. Select any ticker value and select Insert->Break from the menu
    2. Click on any ticker and select Format->Breaks from the menu
    3. Select the <u>Break Header</u> option
    4. Select the <u>Start a New Page</u> option
    5. Select the <u>Repeat the Header on the New Page</u> option

8. Delete the old report header

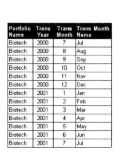
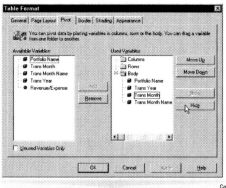

1. Create a report with *Portfolio Name, Trans Year, Trans Month,* and *Trans Month Name*

2. Click on any Trans Month value and sort them A->Z

3. Click on any cell in the table and select <u>Format->Table...</u> from the menu

4. Click on the Pivot Tab to activate it

5. Click on the Trans Month dimension object in the Used Variables list

6. Click on the Hide button to hide Trans Month

7. Click OK

- We can conditionally hide blocks on a report by placing a logical formula in the <u>Hide Block</u> section of the Appearance tab in the Format Block dialog

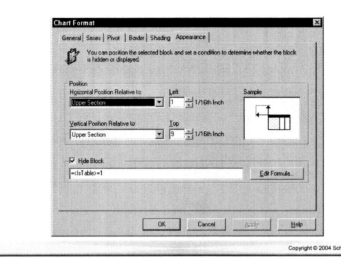

1. Create a report using *Portfolio Name*, *Trans Year*, *Num Transactions*, and *Chart or Table*

    Chart or Table is a special object that will prompt for the block type

2. Create an xTab with Trans Year across the top

3. Create a variable

    Name: IsTable

    Formula: = If UserResponse(DataProvider(<Chart or Table>), "Chart or Table") = "Table" Then 1 Else 0

4. Click anywhere on the xTab and select <u>Format->Crosstab...</u> from the menu.

5. On the Appearance tab, in the Hide Block section, enter the following

    = <IsTable> = 0

6. Click OK

7. Copy the crosstab and convert the copy to a chart

8. Drag the chart on top of the crosstab

9. Click anywhere on the chart and select <u>Format->Chart...</u> from the menu.

10. On the Appearance tab, in the Hide Block section, enter the following

    = <IsTable> = 1

11. Click OK

12. Refresh the query and select chart

Conditional Hiding Sections in a Master-Detail Report

- We can conditionally hide sections in a Master-Detail report by placing a logical formula in the <u>Hide Section Header</u> section of the General tab in the Section Format dialog

1. Create a report using *Portfolio Name*, *Trans Year*, *Trans Quarter*, and *Revenue/Expense*

2. Click on any Portfolio Name and select <u>Format->Set as Master</u> from the menu

3. Click on any Revenue/Expense and select Data->Calculations->Sum

4. Double-click anywhere on the report, in a section

5. Enter the following in the Hide Section Header section

    = <Revenue/Expense> < 0

6. Click OK

Even though the sections are hidden from the report, they are still visible in the Report Manager. Therefore, in companies that use the Report Manager for navigation within master-detail report, you may consider eliminating the unwanted sections in the query. Since the formula in this example uses a summary (Revenue for section less than zero), then a subquery would have to be used to eliminate the unwanted portfolios.

295

Positioning Blocks Relative to Other Blocks

- When a block is placed on a report, it is anchored by its upper-left coordinate
  - When a table grows, because a query has returned more rows, it simply add more rows to the table
  - The table is oblivious to all blocks below it and will continue to grow over any blocks below it.
- We use the Appearance tab of the Format Block dialog to make tables aware of one another.

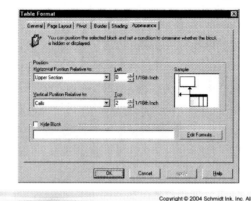

1. Create a report with *Call Portfolio Name*, *Call Year*, and *Num Calls*. Also add the *Call Portfolio Names* condition

2. Select the Biotech portfolio in the prompt dialog

3. Click anywhere on the table and select <u>Format->Table</u> from the menu

4. Enter Calls into the <u>Name</u> field on the General tab

5. Select <u>Insert->Table</u> and place the table just beneath the Calls table

6. Select the <u>Build a query on the universe currently in use</u> option

7. Select *Portfolio Name*, *Trans Year*, and *Revenue/Expense*.
   Drag *Portfolio Name* into the Conditions window. Double-click the In List operator. Double-click the Show List of Prompts operand, and select the Please select Portfolio Names prompt.

8. Click Run and select the Biotech portfolio

9. Click anywhere on the new table and select <u>Format->Table</u> from the menu

10. Enter Transactions into the <u>Name</u> field on the General tab

11. Click on the Appearance tab to activate it

12. Select Calls in the <u>Vertical Position Relative To</u> list

13. Enter a 2 in the <u>Top</u> field

14. Click OK

15. Refresh the report and choose any number of portfolios.

Aligning Blocks with Other Blocks or Cells

- We often need to align the tops or sides of blocks on our reports. We can do this by dragging the blocks until they appear to be aligned. However, the Align Elements dialog is much more accurate and usually quicker.
    - To select more than one block or cell, it is probably best to click on the report, drag the mouse cursor through the blocks, and then release the mouse button.
- After selecting the blocks, select Format->Placement->Alignment... from the menu

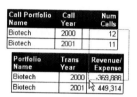 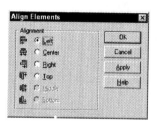

297

Cross Tables

- Crosstabs allow us to present summary information with several different orientations. They are used frequently in reporting and we will explore several behaviors and formats over the next few slides

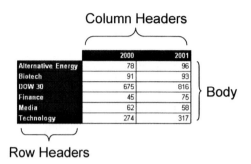

Column Headers

	2000	2001
Alternative Energy	78	96
Biotech	91	93
DOW 30	675	816
Finance	45	75
Media	62	58
Technology	274	317

Body

Row Headers

Cross Tables and Measures

- Typically, users place dimension and detail objects in the headers of cross tables and measures in the body of a cross table. Measures in the body of a cross table will yield summary calculations for the intersection of it's respective row and column headers.
- The following cross tables contain measures in their headers.

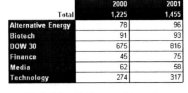

	Total	2000	2001
Alternative Energy	174	78	96
Biotech	184	91	93
DOW 30	1,491	675	816
Finance	120	45	75
Media	120	62	58
Technology	591	274	317

Total in Row Header

	2000	2001
Total	1,225	1,455
Alternative Energy	78	96
Biotech	91	93
DOW 30	675	816
Finance	45	75
Media	62	58
Technology	274	317

Total in Column Header

1. Create a report with *Portfolio Name*, *Trans Year*, and *Num Transactions*
2. Create a crosstab with Trans Year in the column header
3. Copy the block
4. Insert a row header in the first crosstab
5. Copy the measure from the body to the newly inserted header column
6. Insert a column header into the second crosstab
7. Copy the measure from the body to the newly inserted column header

- Another useful cross table trick, is to have no row headers.
  - The trick here is to replace any row headers with hard-coded values that describe the measures in the body of the cross table.

	Alternative Energy	Biotech	DOW 30	Finance	Media	Technology
Num Shares	0	0	0	0	0	0
Num Trans	174	184	1,491	120	120	591
Revenue	$214,664.60	$79,425.70	$1,351,453.00	$67,462.30	-$78,540.30	-$57,269.80

- When this type of technique is combined with other formats, such as breaks, some interesting reports can be created.

	Alternative Energy	Biotech	DOW 30	Finance	Media	Technology
2000 Num Shares	10,200	9,400	90,200	8,700	9,400	28,000
Num Trans	78	91	675	45	62	274
Revenue	-$89,221.30	-$369,888.40	-$4,385,412.50	-$507,100.70	-$465,393.90	-$1,116,767.25

	Alternative Energy	Biotech	DOW 30	Finance	Media	Technology
2001 Num Shares	-10,200	-9,400	-90,200	-8,700	-9,400	-28,000
Num Trans	96	93	816	75	58	317
Revenue	$303,885.90	$449,314.10	$5,736,865.50	$574,563.00	$386,853.60	$1,059,497.45

1. Create a report with *Portfolio Name*, *Trans Year*, *Num Transactions*, *Number Shares*, and *Revenue/Expense*

2. Delete the *Num Transactions* and *Revenue/Expense* columns

3. Create a crosstab with Portfolio Names across the top

4. Select any Trans Year in the row header and type Num Shares

5. Insert two rows under the Num Shares row

6. Type Num Trans and Revenue into the headers

7. Drag the Num Transactions measure from the Report Manager and drop it on the first inserted row

8. Drag the Revenue/Expense measure from the Report Manager and drop it on the last row

To add a break…

1. Insert a column and drag the Trans Year object to the inserted column

2. Click on one of the years in the crosstab and select Insert->Break from the menu

3. Delete the break footer from the report

- With BusinessObjects, we can easily calculate the variance between two columns on a report.
  - To calculate the variance
    - Click on a measure's header cell
    - Hold down the [Ctrl] key and click another measure's header cell
    - Click either of the Variance toolbar buttons.
      - You can also select Data->Calculations->Variance

	2000	2001
Alternative Energy	78	96
Biotech	91	93
DOW 30	675	816
Finance	45	75
Media	62	58
Technology	274	317

	2000	2001	2001-2000	2001-2000
Alternative Energy	78	96	18	23.08 %
Biotech	91	93	2	2.20 %
DOW 30	675	816	141	20.89 %
Finance	45	75	30	66.67 %
Media	62	58	-4	-6.45 %
Technology	274	317	43	15.69 %

=\<Num Transactions\> Where (\<Trans Year\>=2001) –
    \<Num Transactions\> Where (\<Trans Year\>=2000)

=(\<Num Transactions\> Where (\<Trans Year\>=2001) - \<Num Transactions\> Where
    (\<Trans Year\>=2000)) / (\<Num Transactions\> Where (\<Trans Year\>=2000))

1. Create a report with *Portfolio Name*, *Trans Year*, and *Num Transactions*
2. Create a crosstab with Trans Year in the header row
3. Click on the 2001 value in the header
4. Hold down the [Ctrl] key and click on the 2000 header value
5. Click the a-b variance button
6. Click on the 2001 value in the header
7. Hold down the [Ctrl] key and click on the 2000 header value
8. Click the % a-b variance button

End of Course

- If you have worked through all of the examples in this course and listened to all that the instructor had to say, then you must be very fatigued. However, you also must feel very accomplished, for you have done what most other report developers have not. You have explored most of the advance capabilities in BusinessObjects and your level of understanding has greatly increased.

- Thank you very much for taking this course and I hope that it will give you great confidence in BusinessObjects and other applications that may use similar logic and report structures.

Sincerely,
Robert D. Schmidt
RSchmidt@SchmidtInk.com